Let Us Python

First Edition

Yashavant Kanetkar
Aditya Kanetkar

Distributors:

BPB PUBLICATIONS
20, Ansari Road, Darya Ganj
New Delhi-110002
Ph: 23254990/23254991

BPB BOOK CENTRE
376 Old Lajpat Rai Market,
Delhi-110006
Ph: 23861747

MICRO MEDIA
Shop No. 5, Mahendra Chambers, 150
DN Rd. Next to Capital Cinema, V.T.
(C.S.T.) Station,
MUMBAI-400 001
Ph: 22078296/22078297

DECCAN AGENCIES
4-3-329, Bank Street,
Hyderabad-500195
Ph: 24756967/24756400

Published by Manish Jain for BPB Publications, 20, Ansari Road, Darya Ganj, New Delhi-110002 and Printed by him at Repro India Pvt Ltd, Mumbai

Dedicated to
Nalinee & Prabhakar Kanetkar...

About Yashavant Kanetkar

Through his books and Quest Video Courses on C, C++, Java, Python, Data Structures, .NET, IoT, etc. Yashavant Kanetkar has created, molded and groomed lacs of IT careers in the last three decades. Yashavant's books and Quest videos have made a significant contribution in creating top-notch IT manpower in India and abroad.

Yashavant's books are globally recognized and millions of students / professionals have benefitted from them. Yashavant's books have been translated into Hindi, Gujarati, Japanese, Korean and Chinese languages. Many of his books are published in India, USA, Japan, Singapore, Korea and China.

Yashavant is a much sought after speaker in the IT field and has conducted seminars/workshops at TedEx, IITs, IIITs, NITs and global software companies.

Yashavant has been honored with the prestigious "Distinguished Alumnus Award" by IIT Kanpur for his entrepreneurial, professional and academic excellence. This award was given to top 50 alumni of IIT Kanpur who have made significant contribution towards their profession and betterment of society in the last 50 years.

In recognition of his immense contribution to IT education in India, he has been awarded the "Best .NET Technical Contributor" and "Most Valuable Professional" awards by Microsoft for 5 successive years.

Yashavant holds a BE from VJTI Mumbai and M.Tech. from IIT Kanpur. Yashavant's current affiliations include being a Director of KICIT Pvt. Ltd. and KSET Pvt. Ltd.

About Aditya Kanetkar

 Aditya Kanetkar holds a Master's Degree in Computer Science from Georgia Tech, Atlanta. Prior to that, he completed his Bachelor's Degree in Computer Science and Engineering from IIT Guwahati. Aditya started his professional career as a Software Engineer at Oracle America Inc. at Redwood City, California. Currently he works with Microsoft Corp., USA.

Aditya is a very keen programmer since his intern days at Redfin, Amazon Inc. and Arista Networks. His current passion is anything remotely connected to Python, Machine Learning and C# related technologies.

Preface

Programming landscape has changes significantly over the last few years. Python is making inroads into every field that has anything to do with programming. Naturally, Python programming is a skill that one has to acquire, earlier the better.

Newbies who are learning Python as their first programming language will also find the book very simple to understand. Primary credit of this goes to the Python language—it is very simple for the beginner, yet very powerful for the expert who can tap into that power.

Many people learning Python have at least a nodding acquaintance with some programming language. So they are not interested in going through the typical curve of learning the first programming language. Instead, they are looking for something that will get them off the ground quickly. They are looking for similarities and differences in a feature that they have used in other language(s). This book should help them immensely. Instead of explaining a feature with verbose text, wel have mentioned the key points about it as "KanNotes" and explained those points with the help of programs.

If you ask us to name the most important characteristic of this book, we would say simplicity. Be it the code or the text, we have tried to make it as simple as we could. As far as the code is concerned, we wanted to present simple examples that can be easily edited, compiled and run.

You will also notice that very few programming examples in this book are code fragments. We have realized that a program that actually compiles and runs, helps improve one's understanding of a subject a great deal more, than just code fragments.

Simple exercises are exceptionally useful to complete the reader's understanding of a topic. So you will find one at the end of each chapter. Please do attempt them. They will really make you battle-ready.

We have poured my best efforts into these pages. We trust you will find the book useful. We have tried to write a Python book that makes reading it as much fun as the language is. All the best and happy programming!

Yashavant Kanetkar

Aditya Kanetkar

Brief Contents

Contents

1 Introduction to Python

- Python was created by Guido Van Rossum - Fondly known as Benevolent Dictator For Life.

- Python programmers are often called Pythonists or Pythonistas.

- Python was first released in 1991. Today Python interpreters are available for many Operating Systems including Windows and Linux.

- Why people use Python:

  (a) Software Quality:
    - Better than traditional and scripting languages
    - Readable code, hence reusable and maintainable
    - Support for advance reuse mechanisms

  (b) Developer productivity:
    - Much better than statically typed languages
    - Much smaller code
    - Less to type, debug and maintain
    - No lengthy compile and link steps

  (c) Program portability:
    - Programs run unchanged on most platforms
    - Usually need only cut and paste - True even for GUI, DB access, Web programming, OS interfacing, Directory access, etc.

  (d) Support libraries:
    - Strong library support from Text pattern matching to networking
    - Vast collection of third party libraries
    - Libraries for Web site construction, Numeric programming, Game development, Machine Learning etc.

  (e) Component integration:
    - Can invoke C, C++ libraries and Java components
    - Can communicate with frameworks such as COM, .NET
    - Can interact over networks with interfaces like SOAP, XML-RPC, CORBA
    - Popularly used for product customization and extension

  (f) Enjoyment:

- Ease of use
- Built-in toolset
- Programming becomes pleasure than work

- What can be done using Python:
  - System Programming
  - GUI
  - Internet Scripting
  - Component Integration
  - Database Programming
  - Rapid Prototyping
  - Numeric and Scientific Programming
  - Gaming
  - Robotics

- Important features of Python:

  (a) It supports all 3 programming models—Procedural, Object Oriented (OOP) and Functional.

  (b) Its OOP model supports OOP features like Encapsulation, Inheritance, Polymorphism, Operator overloading, Exception handling.

  (c) It is ideal as a scripting tool for OOP languages like C++ and Java.

  (d) With appropriate glue code it can subclass C++, Java, C# classes.

  (e) It is free to use and distribute and is supported by community.

  (f) It is Portable - Standard implementation is written in ANSI C.

  (g) It compiles and runs on every major platform currently in use.

- What sets Python apart?

  (a) Powerful
    - Dynamic typing
    - No variable declaration
    - Automatic allocation and Garbage Collection
    - Supports classes, modules and exceptions
    - Permits componentization and reuse
    - Powerful containers - Lists, Dictionaries, Tuples

  (b) Ready-made stuff
    - For operations like joining, slicing, sorting, mapping, etc.

- Powerful library
- Large collection of 3rd-party utilities

(c) Easy to use

- Type and run
- No compile and link steps
- Interactive programming experience
- Rapid turnaround
- Programs are simpler, smaller and more flexible

- Who uses Python today?
  - Google - In Web search System
  - YouTube - Video Sharing Service
  - Bit-torrent - Peer to Peer file sharing system
  - Hardware testing - Intel, HP, Seagate, IBM, Qualcomm
  - Movie Animation - Pixar, Industrial Light and Magic
  - Financial market forecasting - JP Morgan, Chase, UBS
  - Scientific programming - NASA, FermiLab
  - Commercial Robot Vacuum Cleaners - iRobot
  - Cryptographic & Intelligence analysis - NSA
  - Email Servers - IronPort

- Getting Python source code, binaries, IDE

  (a) Python official website: www.python.org

  (b) Documentation website: www.python.org/doc

  (c) NetBeans IDE for Python: www.netbeans.org

[A] Answer the following:

(a) Mention 5 fields in which Python is popularly used.

(b) Which of the following is not a feature of Python?
- Static typing
- Variable declaration before use
- Destruction of objects after use through destructor
- Run-time error handling through error numbers
- Library support for containers like Lists, Dictionaries, Tuples

2 Python Basics

- Working with Python
- Identifiers and Keywords
- Comments, Indentation and Multi-lining
- Python Types
- Operations and Conversions
- Built-in Functions
- Library Functions
- Programs
- Exercise

What is Python?

- Python is a specification for a language that can be implemented in many different ways. There are many implementations of this specification written in different languages.

- Different popular Python implementations are:

  CPython - is the reference implementation, written in C.
  PyPy - Written in a subset of Python language called RPython.
  Jython - Written in Java.
  IronPython - Written in C#.

- All the implementations are compilers as well as interpreters. The compiler converts the Python program into intermediate bytecode. This bytecode is then interpreted by the interpreter.

Working with Python

- Python programming modes:
  - Interactive mode - used for exploring Python syntax, seek help and debug short programs
  - Script mode - used for writing full-fledged Python programs

- Interactive mode uses IDLE (Python Integrated Development and Learning Environment).

- To use IDLE:
  - Locate it in Windows by typing IDLE and double click it.
  - It will open the Python shell window showing >>> Python shell prompt.
  - Execute the following Python code at this prompt.

    >>> print('Keep calm and bubble on')

  - It displays the message followed by the >>> prompt.

- To execute a Python program in Script mode:
  - Create a new Python project 'Test' in NetBeans or Visual Studio Code.
  - Type the following script in Test.py.

    print('Those who can't laugh at themselves...')
    print('leave the job to others')

- Execute the script using F6.
- On execution it will print the two lines and then you are ready to create another project and another script in it.

- You can execute a script even in IDLE. Go to File | New File and type the program. Execute it from the Run menu.

- Python has evolved over the years. At the time of writing of this book, version 3.7.3 is prevalent.

- You can determine the version installed on your machine through the statements:

import sys
print(sys.version)

Identifiers and Keywords

- Python is a case sensitive language.

- Python identifier is a name used to identify a variable, function, class, module, or other object.

- Rules for creating identifiers:
  - Starts with alphabet or an underscore
  - Followed by zero or more letters, _ , and digits
  - keywords cannot be used as identifier

- All keywords in lowercase.

- Pyhon has 33 keywords that are given below.

False	None	True	and	as
assert	break	class	continue	def
del	eli	else	except	finally
for	from	global	if	import
in	is	lambda	nonlocal	not
or	pass	raise	return	try
while	with	yield		

Comments, Indentation and Multi-lining

- Comments begin with #.

# calculate gross salary
gs = bs + da + hra + ca

OR

gs = bs + da + hra + ca   # calculate gross salary

- Multi-line comments should be written in a pair of ''' or """.

  ''' Purpose: Calculate bonus to be paid
      Team: ResourceManagement
      Author: Sudeep, Date: 18 Jan 2020 '''

- Indentation matters! Don't use it casually. Following code will be reported as error   .

  a = 20
      b = 45

- If statements are long they can be written as multi-lines with each line except the last ending with a \.

  total = physics + chemistry + maths + \
          english + Marathi + history + \
          geography + civics

- Statements within [ ], { }, or ( ) don't need \.

  days = ['Monday', 'Tuesday', 'Wednesday', Thursday',
          'Friday', 'Saturday', 'Sunday']

- No need to define type of a variable. Type is inferred from the context in which the variable is being used.

- Simple variable assignment:

  a = 10
  pi = 3.14
  name = 'Sanjay'

- Multiple variable assignment:

  a = 10 ; pi = 31.4 ; name = 'Sanjay'   # use ; as statement separator
  a, pi, name = 10, 3.14, 'Sanjay'
  a = b = c = d = 5

Python Types

- Python built-in types:

  Basic types - int, float, complex, bool, string, bytes,
  Container types - list, tuple, dict, set
  User-defined - class

- Numbers:

```
int   -  156, 0432, 0x4A3   # decimal, octal, hexadecimal
float - 314.1528, 3.141528e2, 3.141528E2
complex - 3 + 2j, 1 + 4J   # contains real and imaginary part
```

Operations and Conversions

- Arithmetic operators: + - * / % // **

  ```
  % - returns remainder
  ** - exponentiation
  // - returns quotient after discarding fractional part
  ```

- Compound assignments operators: += -= *= /= %= **= //=

  ```
  a **= 3   # same as a = a ** 3
  b %= 10   # same as b = b % 10
  ```

- We can convert one numeric type to another using built-in functions **int( )**, **float( )**, **complex( )** and **bool( )**.

- Type conversions:

  ```
  int(float/numeric string)   # from float/numeric string to int
  int(numeric string, base)   # from numeric string to int in base

  float(int/numeric string)   # from int/numeric string to float
  float(int)   # from int to float

  complex(int / float)   # convert to complex with imaginary part 0
  complex(int / float, int / float)   # convert to complex

  bool(int/float)   # from int/float to True/False (1/0)
  str(int/float/bool)   # converts to string
  chr(int)   # yields character corresponding to int
  ```

Built-in Functions

- Python has many built-in functions that are always available to the program. Some of them are related to mathematical operations.

- Built-in Mathematical functions:

  ```
  abs(x)      # absolute value of x
  pow(x, y)  # value of x raised to y
  min(x1, x2,...)   # smallest argument
  max(x1, x2,...)   # largest argument
  divmod(x, y) # returns a pair(x // y, x % y)
  bin(x)   # binary equivalent
  oct(x)   # octal equivalent
  ```

hex(x) # hexadecimal equivalent
round(x [,n]) # x rounded to n digits after decimal point

Library Functions

- For performing sophisticated mathematical operations we can use the functions present in modules **math, cmath, random, decimal.**

  math - many useful mathematics functions
  cmath - functions for performing operations on complex numbers
  random - functions related to random number generation
  decimal - functions for performing precise arithmetic operations

- Mathematical functions in **math** module:

  pi, e   # constants
  sqrt(x)   # square root of x
  factorial(x)   # factorial of x
  fabs(x)   # absolute value of float x
  log(x)   # natural log of x
  log10(x)   # base-10 logarithm of x
  exp(x)   # e raised to x
  trunc(x)   # truncates to integer
  ceil(x)   # smallest integer >= x
  floor(x)   # largest integer <= x
  modf(x)   # fractional and integer parts of x

- **round( )** function is can round to a specific number of decimal places, whereas **trunc( )**, **ceil( )** and **floor( )** always round to zero decimal places.

- Trigonometric functions in **math** module:

  pi, e # mathematical constants
  degrees(x) # radians to degrees
  radians(x) # degrees to radians
  sin(x)   # sine of x radians
  cos(x)   # cosine of x radians
  tan(x)   # tan of x radians
  sinh(x)   # hyperbolic sine of x
  cosh(x)   # hyperbolic cosine of x
  tanh(x)   # hyperbolic tan of x
  acos(x) # cos inverse of x, in radians
  asin(x) # sine inverse of x, in radians
  atan(x) # tan inverse of x, in radians

hypot(x, y)   # sqrt(x * x + y * y)

- Random number generation functions from **random** module:

  random( )   # random number between 0 and 1
  randint(start, stop)   # random number in the range
  seed(x)   # sets seed used in random number generation logic

- **print( )** function can be used for sending output to screen. There are many variations possible. They will be discussed in chapters to follow.

- To use functions present in a module, we need to import the module using the **import** statement.

Problem 2.1

Demonstrate use of integer types and operators that can be used on them.

Program

```
# use of integer types
print(3 / 4)
print(3 % 4)
print(3 // 4)
print(3 ** 4)

a = 10 ; b = 25 ; c = 15 ; d = 30 ; e = 2 ; f = 3 ; g = 5
w = a + b - c
x = d ** e
y = f % g
print(w, x, y)

h = 99999999999999999
i = 54321
print(h * i)
```

Output

```
0.75
3
0
```

81
20 8 1
543209999999999999945679

Tips

- 3 / 4 doesn't yield 0.

- Multiple statements in a line should be separated using ;

- **print(w, x, y)** prints values separated by a space.

- There is no precision limit on integers.

Problem 2.2

Demonstrate use of float, complex and **bool** types and operators that can be used on them.

Program

```
# use of float
i = 3.5
j = 1.2
print(i % j)

# use of complex
a = 1 + 2j
b = 3 *(1 + 2j)
c = a * b
print(a)
print(b)
print(c)
print(a.real)
print(a.imag)
print(a.conjugate( ))

# use of bool
x = True
print(a)
y = 3 > 4
print(x)
print(y)
```

Output

```
1.1
(1+2j)
(3+6j)
(-9+12j)
1.0
2.0
(1-2j)
(1+2j)
True
False
```

Tips

- % works on floats.

- It is possible to obtain **real** and **imag** part from a complex number.

- On evaluation of a condition it replaced by **True** or **False**.

Problem 2.3

Demonstrate how to convert from one number type to another.

Program

```python
# convert to int
print(int(3.14))  # from float to int
a = int('485')   # from numeric string to int
b = int('768')   # from numeric string to int
c = a + b
print(c)
print(int('1011', 2))  # convert from binary to decimal int
print(int('341', 8))   # convert from octal to decimal int
print(int('21', 16))   # convert from hex to decimal int

# convert to float
print(float(35)) # from int to float
i = float('4.85')   # from numeric string to float
j = float('7.68')   # from numeric string to float
k = i + j
print(k)
```

```
# convert to complex
print(complex(35)) # from int to float
x = complex(4.85, 1.1)   # from numeric string to float
y = complex(7.68, 2.1)   # from numeric string to float
z = x + y
print(z)

# convert to bool
print(bool(35))
print(bool(1.2))
print(int(True))
print(int(False))
```

Output

```
3
1253
11
225
33
35.0
12.53
(35+0j)
(12.53+3.2j)
True
True
1
0
```

Tips

- It is possible to convert a binary numeric string, octal numeric string or hexadecimal numeric string to equivalent decimal integer. Same cannot be done for a **float**.

- While converting to complex if only one argument is used, imaginary part is considered to be 0.

- Any non-zero number (int or float) is treated as **True**. 0 is treated as **False**.

Problem 2.4

Write a program that makes use of built-in mathematical functions.

Program

```
# built-in math functions
print(abs(-25))
print(pow(2, 4))
print(min(10, 20, 30, 40, 50))
print(max(10, 20, 30, 40, 50))
print(divmod(17, 3))
print(bin(64), oct(64), hex(64))
print(round(2.567), round(2.5678, 2))
```

Output

```
25
16
10
50
(5, 2)
0b1000000 0o100 0x40
3 2.57
```

Tips

- **divmod(a, b)** yields a pair **(a // b, a % b)**.

- **bin( )**, **oct( )**, **hex( )** return binary, octal and hexadecimal equivalents.

- **round(x)** assumes that rounding-off has to be done with 0 places beyond decimal point.

Problem 2.5

Write a program that makes use of functions in the math module.

Program

```
# mathematical functions from math module
import math
x = 1.5357
print ( math.pi, math.e)
print(math.sqrt( x))
print(math.factorial(6))
```

```
print(math.fabs(x))
print(math.log(x))
print(math.log10(x))
print(math.exp(x))
print(math.trunc(x))
print(math.floor(x))
print(math.ceil(x))
print(math.trunc(-x))
print(math.floor(-x))
print(math.ceil(-x))
print(math.modf(x))
```

```
3.141592653589793 2.718281828459045
1.2392336341465238
720
1.5357
0.42898630314951025
0.1863063842699079
4.644575595215059
1
1
2
-1
-2
-1
(0.5357000000000001, 1.0)
```

Tips

- **floor( )** rounds down towards negative infinity, **ceil( )** rounds up towards positive infinity, **trunc( )** rounds up or down towards 0.

- **trunc( )** is like **floor( )** for positive numbers.

- **trunc( )** is like **ceil( )** for negative numbers.

Problem 2.6

Write a program that generates float and integer random numbers.

Program

```
# random number operations using random module
import random
random.seed(3)
print(random.random( ))
print(random.random( ))
print(random.randint(10, 100))
```

Output

0.23796462709189137
0.5442292252959519
57

Tips

- It is necessary to import **random** module.

- Even after seeding the randome number generation logic, we get the same set of random numbers on multiple executions of the program. Thus, the numbers are pseudo-random and not true random numbers.

 Exercise

[A] Answer the following:

(a) Write a program that swaps the values of variables **a** and **b**. You are not allowed to use a third variable. You are not allowed to perform arithmetic on **a** and **b**.

(b) Write a program that makes use of trigonometric functions available in math module.

(c) Write a program that generates 5 random numbers in the range 10 to 50. Use a seed value of 6. Make a provision to change this seed value every time you execute the program by associating it with time of execution?

(d) Use **trunc( )**, **floor( )** and **ceil( )** for numbers -2.8, -0.5, 0.2, 1.5 and 2.9 to understand the difference between these functions clearly.

(e) Assume a suitable value for Ramesh's basic salary. His dearness allowance is 40% of basic salary, and house rent allowance is 20% of basic salary. Write a program to calculate his gross salary.

(f) Assume a suitable value for distance between two cities (in km.). Write a program to convert and print this distance in meters, feet, inches and centimeters.

(g) Assume a suitable value for temperature of a city in Fahrenheit degrees. Write a program to convert this temperature into Centigrade degrees and print both temperatures.

[B] How will you perform the following operations:

(a) print imaginary part out of 2 + 3j
(b) Obtain conjugate of 4 + 2j
(c) Convert binary '1100001110' into decimal int
(d) Convert a float value 4.33 into a numeric string
(e) Obtain integer quotient and remainder while dividing 29 with 5
(f) Obtain hexadecimal equivalent of decimal 34567
(g) Round-off 45.6782 to second decimal place
(h) Obtain 4 from 3.556
(i) Obtain 17 from 16.7844
(j) Obtain remainder on dividing 3.45 with 1.22

[C] Which of the following is invalid variable name and why?

BASICSALARY	_basic	basic-hra	#MEAN
group.	422	pop in 2020	over
timemindovermatter	SINGLE	hELLO	queue.
team'svictory	Plot # 3	2015_DDay	

[D] Match the following:

IDLE	\
Escape special character	Python interactive mode
Extension for python script	Python shell prompt
Quickly test a Python feature	Script
complex	Container type
Preserve program	py
Tuple	Basic type
Natural logarithm	log( )
Common logarithm	log10( )

3 Strings

- What are Strings?

- Accessing String Elements

- String Properties

- String Operations

- Programs

- Exercise

What are Strings?

- Python string is a collection of Unicode characters.

- Python strings can be enclosed in single, double or triple quotes.

  'BlindSpot'
  "BlindSpot"
  ' ' 'BlindSpot' ' '
  """Blindspot"""

- Use \ to escape special characters like single quote and double quote.

  'I don\'t like this'
  'He said, \'Let Us Python\'.'

- Multiline strings - 3 ways

  - All but the last line ends with \
  - Enclosed within """some msg """   OR   ' ' 'some msg' ' '
  - ('one msg'
       'another msg')

- If there are characters like ' " or \ within a string, they can be retained in two ways:

  (a) Escape them by preceding them with a \
  (b) Prepend the string with a 'r' indicating that it is a raw string

  msg = 'He said, \'Let Us Python.\''
  msg = r'He said, 'Let Us Python.''

Accessing String Elements

- String elements can be accessed using an index value, starting with 0.

  msg = 'Hello'
  a = msg[0] # yields H
  b = msg[4] # yields o
  c = msg[-0] # yields H, -0 is same as 0
  d = msg[-1] # yields o
  e = msg[-2] # yields l
  f = msg[-5] # yields H

- A sub-string can be sliced out of a string.

  s[start : end] - extract from start to end - 1
  s[start :] - extract from start to end
  s [: end] - extract from start to end - 1
  s [-start :] - extract from -start (included) to end
  s [: -end] - extract from beginning to -end - 1

- Using too large an index reports an error, but using too large index while slicing is handled elegantly.

String Properties

- All strings are objects of built-in type **str**.

  msg = 'Surreal'
  print (type (msg))

  yields <class 'str'>

- Python strings are immutable—they cannot be changed.

  s = 'Hello'
  s[0] = 'M'   # reject, attempt to mutate string
  s = 'Bye'   # s is a variable, it can change

- Strings can be concatenated using +.

  msg3 = ms1 + msg2

- Strings can be replicated during printing

  print ('-', 50)   # prints 50 dashes

String Operations

- Many string functions are available. The have to be used with the syntax string.function( )

  # Content test functions
  isalpha( ) - checks if all characters in string are alphabets
  isdigit( ) - checks if all characters in string are digits
  isalnum( ) - checks if all characters in string are alphabets or digits
  islower( ) - checks if all characters in string are lowercase alphabets
  isupper( ) - checks if all characters in string are uppercase alphabets
  startswith( ) - checks if string starts with a value
  endswith( ) - checks if string ends with a value

  # Conversions
  upper( ) - converts string to uppercase

lower( ) - converts string to uppercase
capitalize( ) - converts string to uppercase
swapcase( ) - swap cases in the string

search and replace
find( ) - searches for a value, returns its position
replace( ) - replace one value with another

lstrip( ) - trim the string from left
rstrip( ) - trim the string from right
split( ) - split the string at a specified separator

- **str( )** function returns a numeric string for its numeric argument

  age = 25
  print ('She is ' + str (age) + ' years old')

- **chr( )** returns a string representing its Unicode value (known as code point). **ord( )** does the reverse.

  ord ('A') # yields 65
  chr (65)   # yields A

p</> Programs

Problem 3.1

Demonstrate how to create simple and multi-line strings and whether a string can change after creation.

Program

```
# simple and multiline strings

msg1 = 'Hoopla'
print ( msg1 )

# escape sequence
msg2 = 'He said, \'Let Us Python\'.'
print ( msg2 )

file1 = 'C:\\temp\\newfile'
print ( file1 )
```

```
# raw string - prepend r
file2 = r'C:\temp\newfile'
print ( file2 )

# multiline strings
# whitespace at beginning of second line becomes part of string
msg3 = 'What is this life if full of care...\
    We have no time to stand and stare'

# enter at the end of first line becomes part of string
msg4 = """What is this life if full of care...
We have no time to stand and stare"""

# strings are concatenated properly. ( ) necessary
msg5 = ( 'What is this life if full of care...'
    'We have no time to stand and stare' )

print ( msg3 )
print ( msg4 )
print ( msg5 )

# string replication during printing
msg6 = 'MacLearn!!'
print ( msg1 * 3 )

# immutability of strings
# Utopia cannot change, msg7 can
msg7 = 'Utopia'
msg8 = 'Today!!!'
msg7 = msg7 + msg8 # concatenation using +
print ( msg7 )

# built-in string function
print ( len ( msg7 ) )
```

Output

Hoopla
He said, 'Let Us Python'.
C:\temp\newfile
C:\temp\newfile
What is this life if full of care...   We have no time to stand and state

What is this life if full of care...
We have no time to stand and state
What is this life if full of care...We have no time to stand and state
HooplaHooplaHoopla
UtopiaToday!!!
14

Tips

- Special characters can be retained in a string by either escaping them or by marking the string as a raw string

- Strings cannot change, but the variables that store them can.

- **len( )** is a built-in function that returns the number of characters present in string.

Problem 3.2

For a given string 'Bamboozled', write a program to obtain the following output :

B a
e d
e d
mboozled
mboozled
mboozled
Bamboo
Bamboo
Bamboo
Bamboo
Bamboozled
Bmoze
Bbzd
Boe
BamboozledHype!
BambooMonger!

Use multiple ways to get any of the above outputs.

Program

```
s = 'Bamboozled'
```

```
# extract B a
print ( s[0], s[1] )
print ( s[-10], s[-9] )
# extract e d
print ( s[8], s[9] )
print ( s[-2], s[-1] )

# extract mboozled
print ( s[2:10])
print ( s[2:] )
print ( s[-8:] )

# extract Bamboo
print ( s[0:6] )
print ( s[:6] )
print ( s[-10:-4] )
print ( s[:-4] )

print ( s[0:10:1] )
print ( s[0:10:2] )
print ( s[0:10:3] )
print ( s[0:10:4] )

s = s + 'Hype!'
print ( s )
s = s[:6] + 'Monger' + s[-1]
print ( s )
```

Tips

- Special characters can be retained in a string by either escaping them or by marking the string as a raw string

- s[4:8] is same as s[4:8:1], where 1 is the default

- s[4:8:2] returns a character, then move forward 2 positions, etc.

Problem 3.3

For the following strings find out which are having only alphabets, which are numeric, which are alphanumeric, which are lowercase, which are uppercase. Also find out whether 'And Quiet flows the Don' begins with 'And' or ends with 'And' :

'NitiAayog'
'And Quiet Flows The Don'
'1234567890'
'Make $1000 a day'

Program

```
s1 = 'NitiAayog'
s2 = 'And Quiet Flows The Don'
s3 = '1234567890'
s4 = 'Make $1000 a day'

print ( 's1 = ', s1 )
print ( 's2 = ', s2 )
print ( 's3 = ', s3 )
print ( 's4 = ', s4 )

# Content test functions
print ( 'check isalpha on s1, s2' )
print ( s1.isalpha( ) )
print ( s2.isalpha( ) )

print ( 'check isdigit on s3, s4' )
print ( s3.isdigit( ) )
print ( s4.isdigit( ) )

print ( 'check isalnum on s1, s2, s3, s4' )
print ( s1.isalnum( ) )
print ( s2.isalnum( ) )
print ( s3.isalnum( ) )
print ( s4.isalnum( ) )

print ( 'check islower on s1, s2' )
print ( s1.islower( ) )
print ( s2.islower( ) )

print ( 'check isupper on s1, s2' )
print ( s1.isupper( ) )
print ( s2.isupper( ) )
```

```
print ( 'check startswith and endswith on s2' )
print ( s2.startswith ( 'And' ) )
print ( s2.endswith ( 'And' ) )
```

Output

```
s1 = NitiAayog
s2 = And Quiet Flows The Don
s3 = 1234567890
s4 = Make $1000 a day
check isalpha on s1, s2
True
False
check isdigit on s3, s4
True
False
check isalnum on s1, s2, s3, s4
True
False
True
False
check islower on s1, s2
False
False
check isupper on s1, s2
False
False
check startswith and endswith on s2
True
False
```

Problem 3.4

Given the following string:

```
'Bring It On'
'   Flanked by spaces on either side   '
'C:\\Users\\Kanetkar\\Documents'
```

write a program to produce the following output using appropriate string functions.

```
BRING IT ON
bring it on
```

Bring it on
bRING iT oN
6
9
Bring Him On
Flanked by spaces on either side
   Flanked by spaces on either side
['C:', 'Users', 'Kanetkar', 'Documents']

Program

```
s1 = 'Bring It On'

# Conversions
print ( s1.upper( ) )
print ( s1.lower( ) )
print ( s1.capitalize( ) )
print ( s1.swapcase( ) )

# search and replace
print ( s1.find ( 'I' ) )
print ( s1.find ( 'On' ) )
print ( s1.replace ( 'It', 'Him' ) )

# trimming
s2 = '   Flanked by spaces on either side   '
print ( s2.lstrip( ) )
print ( s2.rstrip( ) )

# splitting
s3 = 'C:\\Users\\Kanetkar\\Documents'
print ( s3.split ( '\\' ) )
```

 Exercise

[A] Answer the following:

(a) Write a program that generates the following output from the string 'Shenanigan'.

   S h
   a n

enanigan
Shenan
Shenan
Shenan
Shenan
Shenanigan
Seaia
Snin
Saa
ShenaniganType
ShenanWabbite

(b) Write a program to convert the following string

'an inferior lawyer with dubious practices'

into

'An Inferior Lawyer With Dubious Practices'

(c) Write a program to convert the following string

'Light travels faster than sound. This is why some people appear bright until you hear them speak.'

into

'LIGHT travels faster than SOUND. This is why some people appear bright until you hear them speak.'

(d) What will be the output of the following program?

```
s = 'HumptyDumpty'
print ( 's = ', s )
print ( s.isalpha( ) )
print ( s.isdigit( ) )
print ( s.isalnum( ) )
print ( s.islower( ) )
print ( s.isupper( ) )
print ( s.startswith ( 'Hump' ) )
print ( s.endswith ( 'Dump' ) )
```

(e) What is the purpose of a raw string?

(f) What is the difference between the functions **ord( )** and **chr( )**?

(g) Each string is an object of a built-in type called **str**.

(h) If we are to work with individual word in the following string, how will you separate them out:

'The difference between stupidity and genius is that genius has its limits'

4

Control Flow Instructions

- Decision Control Instruction
- Logical Operators
- Conditional Expressions
- Repetition Control Instruction
- *break* and *continue*
- Programs
- Exercise

- Program flow can be controlled using
  - (a) Decision control instruction
  - (b) Repetition control instruction

Decision Control Instruction

- Three ways for taking decisions in a program:

if condition :
    statement1
    statement2
	if condition :
	    statement1
	    statement2
	else :
	    statement3
	    statement4
		if condition1 :
		    statement1
		    statement2
		elif condition2 :
		    statement3
		elif condition3 :
		    statement4
		else :
		    statement5

Note the : after **if, else, elif**. It is compulsory.
Note the indentation of statements in **if** block, **else**, block, **elif** block.

- Condition is built using relation operators <, >, <=, >=, ==, !=.

- An **if-else** statement can be nested inside another **if-else** statement.

- **a = b** is assignment, **a == b** is comparison.

- In **if (a == b == c)** result of **a == b** is compared with **c**.

- If a condition is true it is replaced by 1, if it false it is replaced by 0.

- Any non-zero number is true, 0 is false.

Logical Operators

- More complex decision making can be done using logical operators **and, or** and **not**.

- Conditions can be combined using **and** and **or**.

  cond1 and cond2 - returns true if both are true, otherwise false
  cond1 or cond2 - returns true if one of them is true, otherwise false

- Conditions' result can be negated using **not**.

- **not (a <= b)** is same as **(a > b)**. **not (a >= b)** is same as **(a < b)**

- **a = not b** does not change value of **b**.

- **a = not a** means, set **a** to 0 if it is 1, and set it to 1 if it is 0.

- Unary operator - needs only 1 operand. Ex. **not**

- Binary operator - needs 2 operands. Ex. + - * / % < > etc.

Conditional Expressions

- Python supports one additional decision-making entity called a conditional expression (also called conditional operator or ternary operator).

  <expr1> if <relational expression> else <expr2>

  <relational expression> is evaluated first. If it is true, the expression evaluates to <expr1>. If it is false, the expression evaluates to <expr2>.

- Examples of condition expressions:

  age = 15
  status = 'minor' if age < 18 else 'adult'   # sets minor

  sunny = False
  print('Let's go to the', 'beach' if sunny else 'room')

  humidity = 76.8
  setting = 25 if humidity > 75 else 28   # sets 25

Repetition Control Instruction

- There are two types of repetition control instructions:
  (a) while
  (b) for

- **while** is used to repeatedly execute instructions as long as expression is true. It has two forms:

while condition :	while condition :
statement1	statement1
statement2	statement2
	else :
	statement3
	statement4

else block is executed when **condition** fails.

- **for** is used to iterate over elements of a sequence such as string, tuple or list. It has two forms:

for var in list :	for var in list :
statement1	statement1
statement2	statement2
	else :
	statement3
	statement4

  During each iteration **var** is assigned the next value form the list. **else** block is executed when items in the **list** get exhausted.

- List is a sequence type. It can contain a list of usually similar items.

  ```
  for animal in ['Cat', 'Dog', 'Tiger', 'Lion', 'Leopard'] :
      print( animal + ' ' + str(len(animal)))  # prints animal and length
  ```

- A for loop can be used to generate a **list** of numbers using the built-in **range( )** function.

  range(10) - generates numbers from 0 to 9
  range(10,20) - generates numbers from 10 to 19
  range(10,20,2) - generates numbers from 10 to 19 in steps of 2
  range(20,10,-3) - generates numbers from 20 to 9 in steps of -3

break and *continue*

- **break** and **continue** statements can be used with **while** and **for**.

- **break** statement terminates the loop without executing the **else** block.

- **continue** statement skips the rest of the statements in the block and continues with the next iteration of the loop.

pass Statement

- **pass** statement is intended to do nothing on execution. Hence it is often called a no-op instruction.

- It is often used as a placeholder for unimplemented code in an if, loop, function or class. This is not a good use of **pass**. Instead you should use ... in its place. If you use **pass** it might make one believe that you actually do not intend to do anything in the if/loop/function/class.

Problem 4.1

While purchasing certain items, a discount of 10% is offered if the quantity purchased is more than 1000. If quantity and price per item are input through the keyboard, write a program to calculate the total expenses.

Program

```
qty = int(input('Enter value of quantity: '))
price = float(input('Enter value of price: '))
if qty > 1000 :
    dis = 10
else :
    dis = 0
totexp = qty * price - qty * price * dis / 100
print('Total expenses = Rs. ' + str(totexp))
```

Output

Enter value of quantity: 1200
Enter value of price: 15.50
Total expenses = Rs. 16740.0

Tips

- **input( )** returns a string, so it is necessary to convert it into int or float suitably.

- If we do not do the conversion, **qty > 1000** will throw an error as a string cannot be compared with an int.

- **str( )** should be used to convert **totexp** to string before doing concatenation using +.

Problem 4.2

In a company an employee is paid as under:

If his basic salary is less than Rs. 1500, then HRA = 10% of basic salary and DA = 90% of basic salary. If his salary is either equal to or above Rs. 1500, then HRA = Rs. 500 and DA = 98% of basic salary. If the employee's salary is input through the keyboard write a program to find his gross salary.

Program

```
bs = int(input('Enter value of bs: '))
if bs > 1000 :
    hra = bs * 15 /100
    da = bs * 95 / 100
    ca = bs * 10 / 100
else:
    hra = bs * 10 / 100
    da = bs * 90 / 100
    ca = bs * 5 / 100
gs = bs + da + hra + ca
print('Gross Salary = Rs. ' + str(gs))
```

Tips

- **if** block and **else** block can contain multiple statements in them, suitably indented.

Problem 4.3

Percentage marks obtained by a student are input through the keyboard. The student gets a division as per the following rules:

Percentage above or equal to 60 - First division
Percentage between 50 and 59 - Second division
Percentage between 40 and 49 - Third division
Percentage less than 40 - Fail

Write a program to calculate the division obtained by the student.

Program

```
per = int(input('Enter value of percentage: '))
if per >= 60 :
    print('First Division')
elif per >= 50 :
    print('Second Division')
elif per >= 40 :
    print('Third Division')
else :
    print('Fail')
```

Output

Enter value of percentage: 55
Second Division

Problem 4.4

A company insures its drivers in the following cases:

- If the driver is married.
- If the driver is unmarried, male & above 30 years of age.
- If the driver is unmarried, female & above 25 years of age.

In all other cases, the driver is not insured. If the marital status, sex and age of the driver are the inputs, write a program to determine whether the driver should be insured or not.

Program

```python
ms = input('Enter marital status: ')
s = input('Enter sex: ')
age = int(input('Enter age: '))
if ( ms == 'm' ) or ( ms == 'u' and s == 'm' and age > 30 ) \
    or ( ms == 'u' and s == 'f' and age > 25 ) :
    print('Insured')
else :
    print('Not Insured')
```

Output

Enter marital status: u
Enter sex: m
Enter age: 23
Not Insured

Problem 4.5

Write a program that receives 3 sets of values of p, n and r and calculates simple interest for each.

Program

```python
i = 1
while i <= 3 :
    p = float(input('Enter value of p: '))
    n = int(input('Enter value of n: '))
```

```
r = float(input('Enter value of r: '))
si = p * n * r / 100
print('Simple interest = Rs. ' + str (si))
i = i + 1
```

Output

```
Enter value of p: 1000
Enter value of n: 3
Enter value of r: 15.5
Simple interest = Rs. 465.0
Enter value of p: 2000
Enter value of n: 5
Enter value of r: 16.5
Simple interest = Rs. 1650.0
Enter value of p: 3000
Enter value of n: 2
Enter value of r: 10.45
Simple interest = Rs. 626.9999999999999
```

Problem 4.6

Write a program that prints numbers from 1 to 10 using an infinite loop. All numbers should get printed in the same line.

Program

```
i = 1
while 1 :
    print(i, end=' ')
    i += 1
    if i > 10 :
        break
```

Output

1 2 3 4 5 6 7 8 9 10

Tips

- **while 1** creates an infinite loop, as 1 is non-zero, hence true.

- Replacing 1 in **while 1** with any non-zero number in place of 1 will create an infinite loop.

- **end=' '** in **print( )** prints a space after printing **i** in each iteration. Default value of **end** is newline.

Problem 4.7

Write a program that prints all unique combinations of 1, 2 and 3.

Program

```
i = 1
while i <= 3 :
    j = 1
    while j <= 3 :
        k = 1
        while k <= 3 :
            if i == j or j == k or k == i :
                k += 1
                continue
            else :
                print(i, j, k)
            k += 1
        j += 1
    i += 1
```

Output

```
1 2 3
1 3 2
2 1 3
2 3 1
3 1 2
3 2 1
```

Problem 4.8

Write a program that obtains decimal value of a binary numeric string. Fr example, decimal value of '1111' is 15.

Program

```
b = '1111'
i = 0
while b :
    i = i * 2 + (ord(b[0]) - ord('0'))
```

```
    b = b[1:]
print('Decimal value = ' + str(i))
```

Output

Decimal value = 15

Tips

- **ord(1)** is 49, whereas **ord('0')** is 0.

- **b = b[1:]** strips the first character in **b**.

Problem 4.9

Write a program that receives an integer and determines whether it is a prime number or not.

Program

```
num = int(input('Enter value of num: '))
i = 2
while i <= num - 1 :
    if num % i == 0 :
        print('Not a prime number')
        break
    i += 1
else :
    print('Prime number')
```

Output

Enter value of num: 15
Not a prime number

Tips

- Note the indentation of **else**. It is working for the **while** and not for **if**.

Problem 4.10

Write a program that generates the following output using a **for** loop:

A,B,C,D,E,F,G,H,I,J,K,L,M,N,O,P,Q,R,S,T,U,V,W,X,Y,Z,
z,y,x,w,v,u,t,s,r,q,p,o,n,m,l,k,j,i,h,g,f,e,d,c,b,a,

Program

```
for alpha in range(65,91) :
    print(chr(alpha), end=',')
print( )
for alpha in range(122,96, -1) :
    print(chr(alpha), end=',')
```

Tips

- Unicode values of alphabets A-Z are 65-90. Unicode values of alphabets a-z are 97-122.

- Each output of print statement ends with a comma.

- Empty **print( )** statement positions the cursor at the beginning of the next line.

- indentation of **else**. It is working for the **while** and not for **if**.

Problem 4.11

Suppose there are four flag variables w, x, y, z. Write a program to check in multiple ways whether one of them is true.

Program

```
# Different ways to test multiple flags
w, x, y, z = 0, 1, 0, 1

if w == 1 or x == 1 or y == 1 or z == 1 :
    print('True')

if w or x or y or z :
    print('True')

if any((w, x, y, z)):
    print('True')

if 1 in (w, x, y, z) :
    print('True')
```

Output

True
True

True
True

Tips

- **any( )** is a built-in function that returns True if at least one of its parameters is True.

- Instead of variables, we can pass a string, list, tuple, set or dictionary to **any( )**.

- There is another similar function called **all( )**, which returns true if all parameters are True. This function too can be used with string, list, tuple, set and dictionary.

Problem 4.12

Given a number n we wish to do the following:

If n is positive - print n * n, set a flag to true
If n is negative - print n * n * n, set a flag to true
if n is 0 - do nothing

Is the code given below correct for this logic?

```
n = int(input('Enter a number: '))
if n > 0 :
    flag = true
    print(n * n)
elif n < 0 :
    flag = true
    print(n * n * n)
```

Tips

- This is misleading code. At a later date, anybody looking at this code may feel that **flag = True** should be written outside **if**.

- Better code will be as follows:

```
n = int(input('Enter a number: '))
if n > 0 :
    flag = True
    print(n * n)
elif n < 0 :
    flag = True
    print(n * n * n)
```

```
else :
    pass
```

 **Exercise**

[A] Answer the following:

(a) Write conditional expressions for

- If a < 10 b =20, else b = 30
- Print 'Morning' if time < 12, otherwise print 'Afternoon'

(b) Rewrite the following code snippet in 1 line:

```
x = 3
y = 3.0
if x == y :
    print('x and y are equal')
else :
    print('x and y are not equal')
```

[B] What will be the output of the following programs:

(a)
```
i, j, k = 4, -1, 0
w = i or j or k
x = i and j and k
y = i or j and k
z = i and j or k
print(w, x, y, z)
```

(b)
```
a = 10
a = not not a
print(a)
```

(c)
```
x, y, z = 20, 40, 45
if  x > y and x > z :
    print('biggest = ' + str(x))
elif ( y > x and y > z )
    print('biggest = ' + str(y))
elif ( z > x and z > y )
    print('biggest = ' + str(z))
```

(d)
```
num = 30
k = 100 if num <= 10 else 500
```

```
print(k)
```

[C] Point out the errors, if any, in the following programs:

(a) a = 12.25
     b = 12.52
     if a = b :
         print('a and b are equal')

(b) if ord('X') < ord('x')
         print('Unicode value of X is smaller than that of x')

(c) x = 10
     if x >= 2 then
         print('x')

(d) x = 10 ; y = 15
     if x % 2 = y % 3
         print('Carpathians\n')

(e) x, y = 30, 40
     if x == y :
         print('x is equal to y')
     elseif x > y :
         print('x is greater than y')
     elseif x < y :
         print('x is less than y')

[D] If a = 10, b = 12, c = 0, find the values of the following expressions:

    a != 6 and b > 5
    a == 9 or b < 3
    not (a < 10)
    not (a > 5 and c)
    5 and c != 8 or !c

[E] Attempt the following:

(a) Write a program to count the number of alphabets and number of digits in the string 'Nagpur-440010'

(b) Any integer is input through the keyboard. Write a program to find out whether it is an odd number or even number.

(c) Any year is input through the keyboard. Write a program to determine whether the year is a leap year or not.

(d) A five-digit number is entered through the keyboard. Write a program to obtain the reversed number and to determine whether the original and reversed numbers are equal or not.

(e) If ages of Ram, Shyam and Ajay are input through the keyboard, write a program to determine the youngest of the three.

(f) Write a program to check whether a triangle is valid or not, when the three angles of the triangle are entered through the keyboard. A triangle is valid if the sum of all the three angles is equal to 180 degrees.

(g) Write a program to find the absolute value of a number entered through the keyboard.

(h) Given the length and breadth of a rectangle, write a program to find whether the area of the rectangle is greater than its perimeter. For example, the area of the rectangle with length = 5 and breadth = 4 is greater than its perimeter.

(i) Given three points **(x1, y1)**, **(x2, y2)** and **(x3, y3)**, write a program to check if all the three points fall on one straight line.

(j) Given the coordinates **(x, y)** of center of a circle and its radius, write a program that will determine whether a point lies inside the circle, on the circle or outside the circle. (Hint: Use **sqrt( )** and **pow( )** functions)

(k) Given a point **(x, y)**, write a program to find out if it lies on the X-axis, Y-axis or on the origin.

(l) A year is entered through the keyboard, write a program to determine whether the year is leap or not. Use the logical operators **and** and **or**.

(m) If the three sides of a triangle are entered through the keyboard, write a program to check whether the triangle is valid or not. The triangle is valid if the sum of two sides is greater than the largest of the three sides.

(n) If the three sides of a triangle are entered through the keyboard, write a program to check whether the triangle is isosceles, equilateral, scalene or right angled triangle.

(o) Write a program to calculate overtime pay of 10 employees. Overtime is paid at the rate of Rs. 12.00 per hour for every hour worked above 40 hours. Assume that employees do not work for fractional part of an hour.

(p) Write a program to find the factorial value of any number entered through the keyboard.

(q) Write a program to print out all Armstrong numbers between 1 and 500. If sum of cubes of each digit of the number is equal to the number itself, then the number is called an Armstrong number. For example, 153 = (1 * 1 * 1) + (5 * 5 * 5) + (3 * 3 * 3).

(r) Write a program to print all prime numbers from 1 to 300.

(s) Write a program to print the multiplication table of the number entered by the user. The table should get displayed in the following form:

29 * 1 = 29
29 * 2 = 58

...

(t) When interest compounds **q** times per year at an annual rate of **r** % for **n** years, the principal **p** compounds to an amount **a** as per the following formula

$$a = p (1 + r / q)^{nq}$$

Write a program to read 10 sets of **p, r, n** & **q** and calculate the corresponding **a**s.

(u) Write a program to generate all Pythagorean Triplets with side length less than or equal to 30.

(v) Population of a town today is 100000. The population has increased steadily at the rate of 10 % per year for last 10 years. Write a program to determine the population at the end of each year in the last decade.

(w) Ramanujan number is the smallest number that can be expressed as sum of two cubes in two different ways. Write a program to print all such numbers up to a reasonable limit.

(x) Write a program to print 24 hours of day with suitable suffixes like AM, PM, Noon and Midnight.

5

Console
Input/Output

- Console Input

- Console Output

- Formatted Printing

- Programs

- Exercise

- Console Input/Output means input from keyboards and output to screen.

Console Input

- Console input can be received using the **input( )** function.

- General form of **input( )** function is

  s = input (prompt)

  prompt is a string that is displayed on the screen, soliciting a value. **input( )** returns a string.

- If 123 is entered as input, '123' is returned.

- **input( )** can be used to receive, 1, or more values.

  # receive full name
  name = input('Enter full name') ;

  # separate first name, middle name and surname
  fname, mname, sname = input('Enter full name: ').split( )

- **split( )** function returns a list which can be iterated over using a **for** loop. We can use this feature to receive multiple values.

  n1, n2, n3 = [int(n) for n in input('Enter three values: ').split( )]
  print(n1+10, n2+20, n3+30)

- **input( )** can be used to receive arbitrary number of values.

  numbers = [int(x) for x in input('Enter values: ').split( )]
  for n in numbers :
      print(n+10)

- **input( )** can be used to receive different types at a time.

  data = input('Enter name, age, salary: ').split(',')
  name = data[0]
  age = int(data[1])
  salary = float(data[2])

Console Output

- **print( )** function **is** used to send output to screen.

- **print( )** function has this form

  print(objects, sep=' ', end='\n', file=sys.stdout, flush=false)

  This means that by default objects will be printed to screen (sys.stdout), separated by space (sep=' ') and last printed object will be followed by a newline (end='\n'). **flush=false** indicates that output stream will not be flushed.

- Python has a facility to call functions and pass keyword-based values as arguments. So while calling **print( )** we can pass specific values for **sep** and **end**. In this case, default values will not be used; instead the values that we pass will be used.

  print(a, b, c, sep=',', end='!') # prints ',' after each value, ! at end
  print(x, y, z, sep='...', end='#') # prints '...' after each value, # at end

Formatted Printing

- There are 3 ways to control the formatting of output:

  (a) Using formatted string literals - easiest
  (b) Using the format( ) method - older
  (c) C printf( ) style - legacy
  (d) Using slicing and concatenation operation - difficult

  Today (a) is most dominantly used method followed by (b).

- Using formatted string (often called fstring) literals:

  r, l, b = 1.5678, 10.5, 12.66
  print(f'radius = {r}')
  print(f'length = {l} breadth ={b}')

  name='Sushant Ajay Raje'
  for n in name.split( ) :
      print(f'{n:10}') # print in 10 columns

- Using **format( )** method:

  r, l, b = 1.5678, 10.5, 12.66
  print('radius = {0} length = {1} breadth ={2}'.format(r, l, b))

  name, age, salary = 'Rakshita', 30, 53000.55
  print('name={0} age={1} salary={2}'.format(name, age, salary))
  print('age={1} salary={2} name={0}'.format(name, age, salary))
  print('name={0:15} salary={1:10}'.format(name, salary))

Problem 5.1

Write a program to receive radius of a circle, and length and breadth of a rectangle in one call to **input( )**. Calculate and print the circumference of circle and perimeter of rectangle.

Program

```
r, l, b = input('Enter radius, length and breadth: ').split( )
radius = int(r)
length = int(l)
breadth = int(b)
circumference = 2 * 3.14 * radius
perimeter = 2 * ( length + breadth )
print(circumference)
print(perimeter)
```

Output

```
Enter radius, length and breadth: 3 4 5
18.84
18
```

Tips

- **input( )** returns a string, so it is necessary to convert it into int or float suitably.

Problem 5.2

Write a program to receive 3 integers using one call to **input( )**. The three integers signify starting value, ending value and step value for a range. The program should use these values to print the number, its square and its cube, all properly right-aligned. Try doing this in multiple ways.

Program

```
start, end, step = input('Enter start, end, step values: ').split( )
# one way
for n in range(int(start), int(end), int(step)) :
```

```
    print(f'{n:>5}{n**2:>7}{n**3:>8}')
print( )

# another way
for n in range(int(start), int(end), int(step)) :
    print('{0:<5}{1:<7}{2:<8}'.format(n, n ** 2, n ** 3))
```

Output

```
Enter start, end, step values: 1 10 2
    1    1    1
    3    9   27
    5   25  125
    7   49  343
    9   81  729

1  1    1
3  9    27
5  25   125
7  49   343
9  81   729
```

Tips

- **{n:>5}** will print n right-justified within 5 columns. Use < to left-justify.

- **{0:<5}** will left-justify 0th parameter in the list within 5 columns. Use > to right-justify.

Problem 5.3

Write a program to maintain names and cell numbers of 4 persons and them print them systematically in a tabular form.

Program

```
contacts = {
            'Dilip' : 9823077892, 'Shekhar' : 6784512345,
            'Vivek' : 9823011245, 'Riddhi' : 9766556779
        }
for name, cellno in contacts.items( ) :
    print(f'{name:15} : {cellno:10d}')
```

Output

Dilip   : 9823077892
Shekhar   : 6784512345
Vivek   : 9823011245
Riddhi   : 9766556779

Problem 5.4

Suppose there are 5 variables in a program—**max, min, mean, sd** and **var**, having some suitable values. Write a program to print these variables properly aligned using multiple fstrings, but one call to **print( )**.

Program

```
min, max = 25, 75
mean = 35
sd = 0.56
var = 0.9
print(
        f'\n{'Max Value:':<15}{max:>10}',
        f'\n{'Min Value:':<15}{min:>10}',
        f'\n{'Mean:':<15}{mean:>10}',
        f'\n{'Std Dev:':<15}{sd:>10}',
        f'\n{'Variance:':<15}{var:>10}' )
```

Output

```
Max Value:         75
Min Value:         25
Mean:              35
Std Deviation:   0.56
Variance:          0.9
```

Problem 5.5

Write a program that prints square root and cube root of numbers from 1 to 10, up to 4 decimal places. Ensure that the output is displayed in separate lines, with number center-justified and square and cube roots, right-justified.

Program

```
import math
width = 10
```

```
precision = 4
for n in range(1, 10) :
    s = math.sqrt(n)
    c = math.pow(n,1/3)
    print(f'{n:^5}{s:{width}.{precision}}{c:{width}.{precision}}')
```

Output

1	1.0	1.0
2	1.414	1.26
3	1.732	1.442
4	2.0	1.587
5	2.236	1.71
6	2.449	1.817
7	2.646	1.913
8	2.828	2.0
9	3.0	2.08

 **Exercise**

[A] Attempt the following:

(a) How will you make the following code more compact?

```
print('Enter ages of 3 persons')
age1 = input( )
age2 = input( )
age3 = input( )
```

(b) Write a program to receive an arbitrary number of floats using one **input( )** statement. Calculate the average of floats received.

(c) Write a program to receive the following using one **input( )** statement.

Name of the person
Years of service
Diwali bonus received

Calculate and print the agreement deduction as per the following formula:

ded = 2 * years of service + bonus * 5.5 / 100
Add 2 to years of service and

(d) What are the default values of **sep** and **end** with regards to **print( )** function?

(e) Write a program to receive 3 integers using one call to **input( )**. The three integers signify starting value, ending value and step value for a range. The program should use these values to print the number, its square root and its cube root, all properly right-aligned. Try doing this in multiple ways.

(f) Write a program to print the following values

a = 12.34, b = 234.39, c = 444.34, d = 1.23, e = 34.67

as shown below

```
a =     12.34
b =    234.39
c =    444.34
d =      1.23
e =     34.67
```

6 Lists

- What are Lists?

- Accessing List Elements

- Basic List Operations

- List Methods

- List Varieties

- List Comprehension

- Programs

- Exercise

What are Lists?

- Container is an entity which contains multiple data items. It is also known as a collection.

- Python has following container data types:

  Lists
  Tuples
  Sets
  Dictionaries

- Container data types are also known as compound data types.

- Though lists can contain dissimilar types, usually they are a collection of similar types.

  animals = ['Zebra', 'Antelope', 'Tiger', 'Chimpanzee', 'Lion']
  ages = [23, 24, 25, 23, 24, 25, 26, 27, 30]

- Items in a list can be repeated, i.e. a list may contain duplicate items.

Accessing List Elements

- Like strings, list items can be accessed using indices. Hence they are also known as sequence types. The index value starts from 0.

  print(animals[1], ages[3])

- Like strings, lists can be sliced

  print(animals[1:3])
  print(ages[3:])

- Entire list can be printed by just using the name of the list.

  l = ['Able', 'was', 'I', 'ere', 'I', 'saw', 'elbA']
  print(l)

- A list of all keywords in Python is also obtained as a list.

  import keyword
  print(keyword.kwlist)

Basic List Operations

- Unlike strings, lists are mutable.

```
animals[2] ='Rhinoceros'
ages[5] = 31
ages[2:5] = [24, 25, 32]
ages[2:5] = [ ]  # delete items 2 to 4
ages[:] = [ ]  # clears all items in the list
```

- Following basic operations can be performed on a list:

```
lst = [12, 15, 13, 23, 22, 16, 17]  # create list
lst = lst + [33, 44, 55]  # concatenation
'a' in ['a', 'e', 'i', 'o', 'u']  # return True since 'a' is present in the list
'z' not in ['a', 'e', 'i', 'o', 'u']  # return True since 'z' is absent in list
del(lst[3])     # delete 3rd item in the list
del(lst[2:5])  # delete items 2 to 4 from the list
del(a[:])       # delete entire list
len(lst)    # return number of items in the list
list('Africa')  # converts the string to a list ['A', 'f', 'r', 'i', 'c', 'a']
max(lst)   # return maximum element in the list
min(lst)   # return minimum element in the list
sorted(lst)   # return sorted list, lst remains unchanged
sum(lst)       # return sum of all elements in the list
```

- It is possible to compare two lists. Comparison is done item by item till there is a mismatch. In following code it would be decided that **a** is less than **b** when 3 and 5 are compared.

```
a = [1, 2, 3, 4]
b = [1, 2, 5]
if a < b :
    print('a is less than b')
elif a == b :
    print('a is equal to b')
else :
    print('b is less than a')
```

List Methods

- List methods are accessed using the syntax **list.function( )**. Some of the commonly needed methods are shown below:

```
lst = [12, 15, 13, 23, 22, 16, 17]  # create list
```

```
lst = lst + [33, 44, 55]  # concatenation
lst.append(22)       # add new item at end
lst.remove(13)       # delete item 13 from list
lst.pop( )           # removes last item in list
lst.pop(3)           # removes 3rd item in the list
lst.insert(3,21)     # insert 21 at 3rd position
lst.reverse( )       # reverse the items in the list
lst.sort( )          # sort items in the list
lst.count(23)        # return number of times 23 appears in lst
idx = lst.index(22)  # return index of item 22
```

List Varieties

- It is possible to create a new list from another.

  birds = ['Parrot', 'Crow', 'Sparrow', 'Eagle']
  b = birds   # copies all items from birds to b

  birds and **b** both are pointing to same list, changing one changes the other.

- It is possible to create a list of lists.

  a = [1, 3, 5, 7, 9]
  b = [2, 4, 6, 8, 10]
  c = [a, b]
  print(c[0][0], c[1][2])   # 0th element of 0th list, 2nd ele of 1st list

- A list may be embedded in another list.

  x = [1, 2, 3, 4]
  y = [10, 20, x, 30]
  print(y) # outputs [10, 20, [1, 2, 3, 4], 30]

- It is possible to unpack a list within a list using the *operator.

  x = [1, 2, 3, 4]
  y = [10, 20, *x, 30]
  print(y)   # outputs [10, 20, 1, 2, 3, 4, 30]

List Comprehension

- List comprehension offers an easy way of creating lists. It consists of brackets containing an expression followed by a **for** clause, and zero or more **for** or **if** clauses.

- So general form of a list comprehension is

lst = [expression for var in sequence [optional for and/or if]]

- Examples of list comprehension:

```
# generate 20 random numbers in the range 10 to 100
a = [random.randint(10, 100) for n in range(20)]
```

```
# from a list delete all numbers having a value between 20 and 50
a = [num for num in a if num > 20 and num < 50]
```

```
# generate square and cube of all numbers between 0 and 10
a = [( x, x**2, x**3) for x in range(10)]
```

```
# generate all unique combinations of 1, 2 and 3
a = [(i, j, k) for i in [1,2,3] for j in [1,2,3] for k in [1, 2, 3] if i != j \
        and j !=k and k != i]
```

```
# flatten a list of lists
arr = [[1,2,3,4], [5,6,7,8]]
b = [n for ele in arr for n in ele]   # one way
c = [*arr[0], *arr[1]]   # one more way
```

p</>Programs

Problem 6.1

Perform the following operations on a list of names.

- Create a list of 5 names - 'Anil', 'Amol', 'Aditya', 'Avi', 'Alka'
- Insert a name 'Anuj' before 'Aditya'
- Append a name 'Zulu'
- Delete 'Avi' from the list
- Replace 'Anil' with 'AnilKumar'
- Sort all the names in the list
- Print reversed sorted list

Program

```
# Create a list of 5 names
names = ['Anil', 'Amol', 'Aditya', 'Avi', 'Alka']
print(names)

# insert a name 'Anuj' before 'Aditya'
names.insert(2,'Anuj')
print(names)
```

```
# append a name 'Zulu'
names.append('Zulu')
print(names)

# delete 'Avi' from the list
names.remove('Avi')
print(names)

# replace 'Anil' with 'AnilKumar'
i=names.index('Anil')
names[i] = 'AnilKumar'
print(names)

# sort all the names in the list
names.sort( )
print(names)

# print reversed sorted list
names.reverse( )
print(names)
```

Output

```
['Anil', 'Amol', 'Aditya', 'Avi', 'Alka']
['Anil', 'Amol', 'Anuj', 'Aditya', 'Avi', 'Alka']
['Anil', 'Amol', 'Anuj', 'Aditya', 'Avi', 'Alka', 'Zulu']
['Anil', 'Amol', 'Anuj', 'Aditya', 'Alka', 'Zulu']
['AnilKumar', 'Amol', 'Anuj', 'Aditya', 'Alka', 'Zulu']
['Aditya', 'Alka', 'Amol', 'AnilKumar', 'Anuj', 'Zulu']
['Zulu', 'Anuj', 'AnilKumar', 'Amol', 'Alka', 'Aditya']
```

Problem 6.2

Perform the following operations on a list of names.

- Create a list of 5 odd numbers
- Create a list of 5 even numbers
- Combine the two lists
- Add prime numbers 11, 17, 29 at the beginning of the combined list
- Report how many elements are present in the list
- Replace last 3 numbers in the list with 100, 200, 300
- Delete all the numbers in the list

- Delete the list

Program

```
# create a list of 5 odd numbers
a = [1, 3, 5, 7, 9]
print(a)

# create a list of 5 even numbers
b = [2, 4, 6, 8, 10]
print(b)
# combine the two lists
a = a + b
print(a)

# add prime numbers 11, 17, 29 at the beginning of the combined list
a = [11, 17, 29] + a
print(a)

# report how many elements are present in the list
num = len(a)
print(num)

# replace last 3 numbers in the list with 100, 200, 300
a[num-3:num] = [100, 200, 300]
print(a)

# delete all the numbers in the list
a[:] = [ ]
print(a)

# delete the list
del a
```

Output

```
[1, 3, 5, 7, 9]
[2, 4, 6, 8, 10]
[1, 3, 5, 7, 9, 2, 4, 6, 8, 10]
[11, 17, 29, 1, 3, 5, 7, 9, 2, 4, 6, 8, 10]
13
[11, 17, 29, 1, 3, 5, 7, 9, 2, 4, 100, 200, 300]
[ ]
```

Problem 6.3

Write a program to implement a Stack data structure. Stack is a Last In First Out (LIFO) list in which addition and deletion takes place at the same end.

Program

```
# stack - LIFO list
s = [ ]   # empty stack
# push elements on stack
s.append(10)
s.append(20)
s.append(30)
s.append(40)
s.append(50)
print(s)

# pop elements from stack
print(s.pop( ))
print(s.pop( ))
print(s.pop( ))

print(s)
```

Output

```
[10, 20, 30, 40, 50]
50
40
30
[10, 20]
```

Problem 6.4

Write a program to implement a Queue data structure. Queue is a First In First Out (LIFO) list, in which addition takes place at the rear end of the queue and deletion takes place at the front end of the queue.

Program

```
import collections
q = collections.deque( )
```

```
q.append('Suhana')
q.append('Shabana')
q.append('Shakila')
q.append('Shakira')
q.append('Sameera')
print(q)

print(q.popleft( ))
print(q.popleft( ))
print(q.popleft( ))
print(q)
```

Output

```
deque(['Suhana', 'Shabana', 'Shakila', 'Shakira', 'Sameera'])
Suhana
Shabana
Shakila
deque(['Shakira', 'Sameera'])
```

Tips

- Lists are not efficient for implementation of queue data structure.

- With lists removal of items from beginning is not efficient, since it involves shifting of rest of the elements by 1 position after deletion.

- Hence for fast additions and deletions, **collections.dequeue** class is preferred.

Problem 6.5

Write a program to generate and store in a list 20 random numbers in the range 10 to 100. From this list delete all those entries which have value between 20 and 50. Print the remaining list.

Program

```
import random

a = [ ]
i = 1
while i <= 15 :
    num = random.randint(10,100)
```

```
    a.append(num)
    i += 1

print(a)

for num in a :
    if num > 20 and num < 50 :
        a.remove(num)

print(a)
```

Output

```
[64, 10, 13, 25, 16, 39, 80, 100, 45, 33, 30, 22, 59, 73, 83]
[64, 10, 13, 16, 80, 100, 33, 22, 59, 73, 83]
```

Tips

- Lists are not efficient for implementation of queue data structure.

- With lists removal of items from beginning is not efficient, since it involves shifting of rest of the elements by 1 position after deletion.

- Hence for fast additions and deletions, **collections.dequeue** class is preferred.

Problem 6.6

Write a program to add two 3 x 4 matrices using

(a) lists
(b) list comprehension

Program

```
mat1 = [[1, 2, 3, 4], [5, 6, 7, 8], [9, 10, 11, 12]]
mat2 = [[1, 2, 3, 4], [5, 6, 7, 8], [9, 10, 11, 12]]
mat3 = [[0, 0, 0, 0], [0, 0, 0, 0], [0, 0, 0, 0]]

# iterate through rows
for i in range(len(mat1)) :
    # iterate through columns
    for j in range(len(mat1[0])) :
        mat3[i][j] = mat1[i][j] + mat2[i][j]
```

```
print(mat3)

mat3 = [[mat1[i][j] + mat2[i][j] for j in range(len(mat1[0]))]
            for i in range(len(mat1))]
print(mat3)
```

Output

[[2, 4, 6, 8], [10, 12, 14, 16], [18, 20, 22, 24]]
[[2, 4, 6, 8], [10, 12, 14, 16], [18, 20, 22, 24]]

Tips

- Nested list comprehension is evaluated in the context of the **for** that follows it.

 **Exercise**

[A] Answer the following:

(a) Write a program to create a list of 5 odd integers. Replace the third element with a list of 4 even integers. Flatten, sort and print the list.

(b) Write a program that generates a list of integer coordinates for all points in the first quadrant from (1, 1) to (5, 5). Use list comprehension.

(c) Write a program to flatten the following list using list comprehension:

mat1 = [[1, 2, 3, 4], [5, 6, 7, 8], [9, 10, 11, 12]]

(d) Write a program using list comprehension to generate a list of numbers in the range 2 to 50 that are divisible by 2 and 4.

(e) Write a program using list comprehension to create a list by multiplying each element in the list by 10.

(f) Suppose there are two lists, each holding 5 strings. Write a program to generate a list using list comprehension that consists of strings that are concatenated by picking corresponding elements from the two lists.

(g) Write a program to generate first 20 Fibonacci numbers using list comprehension.

(h) Suppose a list contains 20 integers generated randomly. Receive a number from the keyboard and report position of all occurrences of this number in the list.

(i) Suppose there are two lists—one contains questions and another contains lists of 4 possible answers for each question. Write a program to generate a list that contains lists of question and its 4 possible answers.

(j) Suppose a list has 20 numbers. Write a program that removes all duplicates from this list.

(k) Write a program to generate two lists using list comprehension. One list should contain first 20 odd numbers and another should contain first 20 even numbers.

(l) Suppose a list contains positive and negative numbers. Write a program to create two lists—one containing positive numbers and another containing negative numbers.

(m) Suppose a list contains 5 strings. Write a program to convert all these strings to uppercase.

(n) Write a program that converts list of temperatures in Fahrenheit degrees to equivalent Celsius degrees.

(o) Write a program to obtain a median value of a list of numbers, without disturbing the order of the numbers in the list.

(p) A list contains only positive and negative integers. Write a program to obtain the number of negative numbers present in the list, without using a loop.

7 Tuples

- What are Tuples?

- Accessing Tuple Elements

- Tuple Operations

- Tuple Varieties

- Tuple Comprehension

- Conversion of List Comprehension to Tuple

- Iterators and Iterables

- *zip( )* Function

- Programs

- Exercise

What are Tuples?

- Tuple is usually a collection of heterogeneous objects enclosed within ( ).

  a = ( )   # empty tuple
  b = (10,)   # tuple with one item. , after 10 is necessary
  c = ('Sanjay', 25, 34555.50)   # tuple with multiple items

  While creating the tuple **b**, if we do not use the comma after 10, **b** is treated to be of type **int**.

- While initializing a tuple, we may drop ( ).

  c = 'Sanjay', 25, 34555.50   # tuple with multiple items
  print(type(c))   # c is of the type tuple

- Tuples are immutable (unlike lists), but they can contain mutable objects like lists.

  # mutable lists, immutable string—all belong to tuple
  s = ([1, 2, 3, 4], [4, 5], 'Ocelot')

- Items in a tuple can be repeated, i.e. tuple may contain duplicate items.

- Tuples are used for handling heterogeneous data and lists for variable length data.

Accessing Tuple Elements

- Like string and list, tuple items too can be accessed using indices, as all of them are sequence types.

  msg = ('Handle', 'Exceptions', 'Like', 'a', 'boss')
  print(msg[1], msg[3])

- Like strings and lists, tuples too can be sliced to yield smaller tuples.

  print(msg[1:3])
  print(msg[3:])

- Entire tuple can be printed by just using the name of the tuple.

  t = ('Subbu', 25, 58.44)
  print(t)

- Like strings and lists, tuples too can be iterated using a **for** loop.

  records = (

  ('Sanjay', 25, 34555.50),
  ('Shailesh', 25, 34555.50),
  ('Subhash', 25, 34555.50)

)
  for n, a, s in records :
     print(n,a,s)

Tuple Operations

- Unlike lists, tuples are immutable.

  msg = ('Fall', 'In', 'Line')
  msg[0] ='FALL' # error
  msg[1:3] = ('Above', 'Mark') # error

- Common tuple operations are shown below:

  t = (12, 15, 13, 23, 22, 16, 17) # create tuple
  t = t + (3.3, 4.4, 5.5) # concatenation
  12 in t # return True since 12 is present in tuple t
  22 not in t # return False since 22 is present in tuple t
  len(t) # return number of items in tuple t
  tuple('Africa') # converts the string to a tuple ('A', 'f', 'r', 'i', 'c', 'a')
  max(t) # return maximum element in tuple t
  min(t) # return minimum element in tuple t
  sorted(t) # return sorted tuple, t remains unchanged
  sum(t)   # return sum of all elements in tuple t
  t.index(15) # return index of item 15
  t.count(15) # returns number of times 15 occurs in tuple t

  Since tuples are immutable operations like append, remove, insert, reverse, sort, del do not work with tuple.

- It is possible to compare two tuples. Comparison is done item by item till there is a mismatch. Some sample comparisons are shown below.

  (10, 20, 30) < (10, 30, 20)
  (10, 20) < (10, 20, -10)
  (32, 42, 52) == (32.0, 42.0, 52.0)

Tuple Varieties

- It is possible to create a tuple of tuples.

```
a = (1, 3, 5, 7, 9)
b = (2, 4, 6, 8, 10)
c = (a, b)
print(c[0][0], c[1][2])  # 0th element of 0th tuple, 2nd ele of 1st tuple
```

- A tuple may be embedded in another tuple.

```
x = (1, 2, 3, 4)
y = (10, 20, x, 30)
print(y)  # outputs (10, 20, (1, 2, 3, 4), 30)
```

- It is possible to unpack a tuple within a tuple using the *operator.

```
x = (1, 2, 3, 4)
y = (10, 20, *x, 30)
print(y)   # outputs (10, 20, 1, 2, 3, 4, 30)
```

Tuple Comprehension

- There is no such thing as a tuple comprehension.

- A comprehension works by looping or iterating over items and assigning them to a container. This container cannot be a tuple as tuple being immutable is unable to receive assignments.

- Though a tuple is iterable and seems like an immutable list, it's really the Python equivalent of a C struct.

Conversion of List Comprehension to Tuple

- We can convert a list to a tuple using the **tuple( )** function. The list may be a normal list or one generated through list comprehension.

```
a = tuple([10, 20, 30, 40, 50])
b = tuple([(x, x**2, x**3) for x in range(10)])
```

Iterators and Iterables

- Iterator is an object that can be iterated upon—i.e. an object that will return data, one element at a time.

- Iterators are implemented in for loops, comprehensions, generators etc.

- An object is called iterable if we can get an iterator from it. Containers string, list, tuple are iterables.

zip( ) Function

- **zip( )** function receives 0 or more iterable objects and returns an iterator of tuples based on them.

  words = ['A coddle called Molly']
  numbers = [10, 20, 30, 40]
  ti1 = zip( )   # returns an empty iterator
  ti2 = zip(words) # returns an iterator of tuples, each containing 1 ele

  # returns an iterator of tuples, each tuple containing 2 elements
  ti2 = zip(words, numbers)

- If two iterables are passed to zip, one containing 4 and other containing 6 elements, the returned iterator has 4 (shorter iterable) tuples.

- A list can be generated from the iterator of tuples returned by zip.

  l = list(ti2)

- The values can be unzipped from the list into tuples using *.

  w, n = zip(*l)

Problem 7.1

Create 3 lists—a list of names, a list of ages and a list of salaries. Generate and print a list of tuples containing name, age and salary from the 3 lists. From this list generate 3 tuples—one containing all names, another containing all ages and third containing all salaries.

Program

```
names = ['Amol', 'Anil', 'Akash']
ages = [25, 23, 27]
salaries= [34555.50, 40000.00, 450000.00]

# create iterator of tuples
it = zip(names, ages, salaries)

# build list by iterating the iterator object
lst = list(it)
print(lst)
```

```
# unzip the list into tuples
n, a, s = zip(*lst)
print(n)
print(a)
print(s)
```

Output

[('Amol', 25, 34555.5), ('Anil', 23, 40000.0), ('Akash', 27, 450000.0)]
('Amol', 'Anil', 'Akash')
(25, 23, 27)
(34555.5, 40000.0, 450000.0)

Problem 7.2

Write a program to obtain transpose of a 3 x 4 matrix.

Program

```
mat = [[1, 2, 3, 4], [5, 6, 7, 8], [9, 10, 11, 12]]
ti = zip(*mat)
lst = list(ti)
print(lst)
```

Output

[(1, 5, 9), (2, 6, 10), (3, 7, 11), (4, 8, 12)]

Tips

- **mat** contains a list of lists. These can be accessed using either **mat[0]**, **mat[1]** and **mat[2]** or simply ***mat**.

- **zip(*mat)** receives three lists and returns an iterator of tuples, each tuple containing 3 elements.

- The iterator returned by **zip( )** is used by **list( )** to generate the list.

Problem 7.3

Write a program to multiply two matrices x(2 x 3) and y(2, 2) using list comprehension.

Program

```
x = [
        [1, 2, 3],
        [4, 5, 6]
    ]
y = [
        [11, 12],
        [21, 22],
        [31, 32]
    ]

l1 = [ xrow for xrow in x ]
print(l1)

l2 = [ (xrow, ycol) for ycol in zip(*y) for xrow in x ]
print(l2)

l3 = [[sum(a * b for a,b in zip(xrow,ycol)) for ycol in zip(*y)]for xrow in x]
print(l3)
```

Output

```
[[1, 2, 3], [4, 5, 6]]
[([1, 2, 3], (11, 21, 31)), ([4, 5, 6], (11, 21, 31)), ([1, 2, 3], (12, 22, 32)),
    ([4, 5, 6], (12, 22, 32))]
[[146, 152], [335, 350]]
```

Tips

- To make it easy for you to understand the list comprehension, I have built it in 3 parts. Follow them by checking their output.

Problem 7.4

Pass a tuple to the **divmod( )** function and obtain the quotient and the remainder.

Program

```
result = divmod(17,3)
print(result)
t = ( 17, 3 )
result = divmod(*t)
```

print(result)

Output

(5, 2)
(5, 2)

Tips

- If we pass **t** to **divmod( )** an error is reported. We have to unpack the tuple into two distinct values and then pass them to **divmod( )**.

- **divmod( )** returns a tuple consisting of quotient and remainder.

Problem 7.5

Suppose we have a list of 5 integers and a tuple of 5 floats. Can we zip them and obtain an iterator. If yes, how?

Program

```
integers = [ 10, 20, 30, 40, 50]
floats = (1.1, 2.2, 3.3, 4.4, 5.5)

ti = zip(integers, floats)
lst = list(ti)
for i, f in lst :
    print(i, f)
```

Output

10 1.1
20 2.2
30 3.3
40 4.4
50 5.5

Tips

- Any iterables can be passed to a **zip( )** function.

 Exercise

[A] Answer the following:

(a) Suppose a date is represented as a tuple (d, m, y). Write a program to create two date tuples and find the number of days between the two dates.

(b) Create a list of tuples. Each tuple should contain an item and its price in float. Write a program to sort the tuples in descending order by price.

(c) Store the data about shares held by a user as tuples containing the following information about shares:

Share name
Date of purchase
Cost price
Number of shares
Selling price

Write a program to determine:

- Total cost of the portfolio.
- Total amount gained or lost.
- Percentage profit made or loss incurred.

(d) Write a program to unzip a list of tuples into individual lists.

[(10, 20, 30), (150.55, 145.60, 157.65), ('A1', 'B1', 'C1')]

(e) Write a program to remove empty tuple from a list of tuples.

(f) Write a program to create following 3 lists:

- a list of names
- a list of roll numbers
- a list of marks

Generate and print a list of tuples containing name, roll number and marks from the 3 lists. From this list generate 3 tuples—one containing all names, another containing all roll numbers and third containing all marks.

(g) What will be the output of the following program:

```
x = [ [1, 2, 3, 4], [4, 5, 6, 7] ]
y = [ [1, 1], [2, 2], [3, 3], [4, 4] ]
```

```
l1 = [ xrow for xrow in x ]
print(l1)
l2 = [ (xrow, ycol) for ycol in zip(*y) for xrow in x ]
print(l2)
```

8 Sets

- What are Sets?

- Accessing Set Elements

- Set Operations

- Set Functions

- Mathematical Set Operations

- Updating Set Operations

- Programs

- Exercise

What are Sets?

- Sets are like lists, with an exception that they do not contain duplicate entries.

    a = ( )   # empty set, note the use of ( ) instead of { }
    b = {20}   # set with one item
    c = {'Sanjay', 25, 34555.50}   # set with multiple items
    d = {10, 10, 10, 10}   # only one 10 gets stored

- Set is an unordered collection. Hence order of insertion is not same as the order of access.

    c = {15, 25, 35, 45, 55}
    print(c)   # prints {35, 45, 15, 55, 25}

- **set( )** function can be used to convert a string, list or tuple into a set.

    l = [10, 20, 30, 40, 50]
    t = ('Sanjay', 25, 450000.00)
    s = 'Oceania'
    s1 = set(l)
    s2 = set(t)
    s3 = set(s)

    While creating a set using **set( )**, repetitions are eliminated.

- Sets like lists are mutable. Their contents can be changed.

- A set cannot contain a set embedded in it.

Accessing Set Elements

- Being an unordered collection, items in a set cannot be accessed using indices.

- Sets cannot be sliced using [ ].

- Entire set can be printed by just using the name of the set.

    s = {'Subbu', 25, 58.44}
    print(s)

- Like strings, lists and tuples, sets too can be iterated over using a **for** loop.

```
s = { 12, 15, 13, 23, 22, 16, 17 }
for ele in s :
    print(ele)
```

Set Operations

- Built-in functions and common set operations are shown below:

```
s = {12, 15, 13, 23, 22, 16, 17}  # create set
12 in s  # return True since 12 is present in set s
22 not in s   # return False since 22 is present in sets
len(s)    # return number of items in set s
max(s)  # return maximum element in set s
min(s)   # return minimum element in set s
sorted(s)  # return sorted set, s remains unchanged
sum(s)      # return sum of all elements in set s
```

- It is possible to unpack a set using the *operator.

```
x = {1, 2, 3, 4}
print(*x)  # outputs 1, 2, 3, 4
```

Set Functions

- Following functions can be used on sets:

```
s = {12, 15, 13, 23, 22, 16, 17}
t = {'A', 'B', 'C'}
s.update(t)   # adds elements of t to s
s.add('Hello') # adds 'Hello' to s
s.remove(15)  # deletes 15 from s
s.discard(101)  # remove(101) would raise error, discard(101) won't
s.clear( )  # removes all elements
```

Mathematical Set Operations

- Following union, intersection and difference operations can be carried out on sets:

```
# sets
engineers = {'Vijay', 'Sanjay', 'Ajay', 'Sujay', 'Dinesh'}
managers = {'Aditya', 'Sanjay'}

# union - all people in both categories
print(engineers | managers)

# intersection - who are engineers and managers
print(engineers & managers)
```

```
# difference - engineers who are not managers
print(engineers - managers)
```

```
# difference - managers who are not engineers
print(managers - engineers )
```

```
# symmetric difference - managers who are not engineers
# and engineers who are not managers
print(managers ^ engineers )
```

```
a = {1, 2, 3, 4, 5}
b = {2, 4, 5}
print(a >= b)   # prints True as a is superset of b
print(a <= b)   # prints False as a is not a subset of b
```

Updating Set Operations

- Mathematical set operations can be extended to update an existing set.

```
a |= b    # update a with the result of a | b
a &= b    # update a with the result of a & b
a -= b    # update a with the result of a - b
a ^= b    # update a with the result of a ^ b
```

Set Comprehension

- Like list comprehensions, set comprehensions offer an easy way of creating sets. It consists of braces containing an expression followed by a **for** clause, and zero or more **for** or **if** clauses.

- So general form of a set comprehension is

  s = {expression for var in sequence [optional for and/or if] }

- Examples of set comprehension:

```
# generate a set containing square of all numbers between 0 and 10
a = {x**2 for x in range(10)}
```

```
# from a set delete all numbers between 20 and 50
a = {num for num in a if num > 20 and num < 50}
```

p</>Programs

Problem 8.1

What will be the output of the following program?

a = {10, 20, 30, 40, 50, 60, 70}

```
b = {33, 44, 51, 10, 20,50, 30, 33}
print(a | b)
print(a & b)
print(a - b)
print(b - a)
print(a ^ b)
print(a >= b)
print(a <= b)
```

Output

```
{33, 70, 40, 10, 44, 50, 51, 20, 60, 30}
{10, 50, 20, 30}
{40, 60, 70}
{33, 51, 44}
{33, 70, 40, 44, 51, 60}
False
False
```

Problem 8.2

What will be the output of the following program?

```
a = {1, 2, 3, 4, 5, 6, 7}
b = {1, 2, 3, 4, 5, 6, 7}
c = {1, 2, 3, 4, 5, 6, 7}
d = {1, 2, 3, 4, 5, 6, 7}
e = {3, 4, 1, 0, 2, 5, 8, 9}
a |= e
print(a)
b &= e
print(b)
c -= e
print(c)
d ^= e
print(d)
```

Output

```
{0, 1, 2, 3, 4, 5, 6, 7, 8, 9}
{1, 2, 3, 4, 5}
{6, 7}
{0, 6, 7, 8, 9}
```

Problem 8.3

Write a program to carry out the following operations on the given set

s = { 10, 2, -3, 4, 5, 88 }

- number of items in set s
- maximum element in set s
- minimum element in set s
- sum of all elements in set s
- obtain a new sorted set from s, set s remaining unchanged
- report whether 100 is an element of set s
- report whether -3 is an element of set s

Program

```
s = { 10, 2, -3, 4, 5, 88 }
print(len(s))
print(max(s))
print(min(s))
print(sum(s))
t = sorted(s)
print(t)
print ( 100 in s )
print ( -3 not in s )
```

Output

```
6
88
-3
106
[-3, 2, 4, 5, 10, 88]
False
False
```

Problem 8.4

What will be the output of the following program?

Program

```
l = [10, 20, 30, 40, 50]
t = ('Sundeep', 25, 79.58)
s = 'set theory'
s1 = set(l)
```

```
s2 = set(t)
s3 = set(s)
print(s1)
print(s2)
print(s3)
```

Output

{40, 10, 50, 20, 30}
{25, 79.58, 'Sundeep'}
{'h', 's', 't', 'y', ' ', 'r', 'e', 'o'}

 **Exercise**

[A] Answer the following:

(a) A set contains names which begin either with A or with B. write a program to separate out the names into two sets, one containing names beginning with A and another containing names beginning with B.

(b) Create an empty set. Write a program that adds five new names to this set, modifies one existing name and deletes two existing names in it.

(c) What is the difference between the two set functions—**discard( )** and **remove( )**.

(d) Write a program to create a set containing 10 randomly generated numbers in the range 15 to 45. Count how many of these numbers are less than 30. Delete all numbers which are greater than 35.

(e) What do the following set operators do?

|, &, ^, -

(f) What do the following set operators do?

|=, &=, ^=, -=

(g) Which operator is used for determining whether a set is a subset of another set?

(h) What will be the output of the following program?

s = { 'Mango', 'Banana', 'Guava', 'Kiwi'}

```
s.clear( )
print(s)
del(s)
print(s)
```

(i) Which of the following is the correct way to create an empty set?

```
s1 = ( )
s2 = { }
```

What are the types of s1 and s2? How will you confirm the type?

9 Dictionaries

- What are Dictionaries?

- Accessing Dictionary Elements

- Dictionary Operations

- Dictionary Functions

- Nested Dictionary

- Programs

- Exercise

What are Dictionaries?

- Dictionary is a collection of key-value pairs. Unlike sequence types they are indexed by keys.

- Dictionaries are also known as maps or associative arrays.

- Keys in a dictionary must be unique and immutable. So strings or tuples can be used as keys.

- Ways to create dictionary:

  ```
  a = { }  # empty dictionary
  b = { 'A101' : 'Amol', 'A102' : 'Anil', 'B103' : 'Ravi' }
  lst = [12, 13, 14, 15, 16]
  e = dict.fromkeys(lst, 25)  # all values set to 25
  ```

- Though key values are unique, different keys may have same value.

Accessing Dictionary Elements

- Dictionary elements can be accessed using key as an index.

  ```
  b = { 'A101' : 'Dinesh', 'A102' : 'Shrikant', 'B103' : 'Sudhir' }
  print(b['A102'])   # prints value for key 'A101'
  print(b)   # prints all key-value pairs
  ```

- Dictionary can be iterated over in three ways:

  ```
  # iterate over key-value pairs
  for k, v in courses.items( ) :
      print(k, v)

  # iterate over keys
  for k in courses.keys( ) :
      print(k)

  # iterate over keys - shorter way
  for k in courses :
      print(k)

  # iterate over values
  for v in courses.values( ) :
      print(v)
  ```

Dictionary Operations

- Dictionaries are mutable.

- Dictionaries are mutable. So we can perform add/delete/modify operations on a dictionary.

  courses = { 'CS101' : 'CPP', 'CS102' : 'DS', 'CS201' : 'OOP',
              'CS226' : 'DAA', 'CS601' : 'Crypt', 'CS442' : 'Web' }

  # add, modify, delete
  courses['CS444'] = 'Web Services' # add new key value pair
  courses['CS201'] = 'OOP Using java' # modify value for a key
  del(courses['CS102']) # delete a key-value pair
  del(courses) # delete dictionary object

- Other common dictionary operations are shown below:

  len(courses) # return number of key-value pairs
  max(courses) # return maximum key value
  min(courses) # return minimum key value

  # existence
  'ME101' in courses # returns True is ME101 is present in courses
  'CE102' not in courses # returns True is CE102 is absent in courses

  # obtain keys in insertion order
  lst = list(courses.keys( ))
  # obtain keys in insertion order - shorter way
  lst = list(courses)

  # obtain sorted list of keys
  lst = sorted(courses.keys( ))
  # obtain sorted list of keys - shorter way
  lst = sorted(courses)

Dictionary Functions

- There are many dictionary methods. Many of the operations performed by them can also be performed by the built-in functions. The useful dictionary functions are shown below:

  courses.clear( ) # clears all dictionary entries
  courses.update(d1) # adds dictionary entries in d1 to courses

Nested Dictionary

- Dictionaries can be nested.

```
contacts = {
                'Anil': { 'DOB' : '17/11/98', 'Favorite' : 'Igloo' },
                'Amol': { 'DOB' : '14/10/99', 'Favorite' : 'Tundra' },
                'Ravi': { 'DOB' : '19/11/97', 'Favorite' : 'Artic' }
           }
```

Dictionary Comprehension

- Genreral form:

    dict_var = {key:value for (key, value) in dictonary.items( )}

- Examples:

    d = {'a': 1, 'b': 2, 'c': 3, 'd': 4, 'e': 5}

    # obtain dictionary with each value cubed
    d1 = {k : v ** 3 for (k, v) in d.items( )}
    print(d1)

    # obtain dictionary with each value cubed if value > 3
    d2 = {k : v for (k, v) in d.items( ) if v > 3}
    print(d2)

    # Identify odd and even entries in the dictionary
    d3 = {k : ('Even' if v % 2 == 0 else 'Odd') for (k, v) in d.items( )}

Problem 9.1

Create a dictionary called **students** containing names and ages. Copy the dictionary into **stud**. Empty the **students** dictionary, as **stud** continues to hold the data.

Program

```
students = { 'Anil' : 23, 'Sanjay' : 28, 'Ajay' : 25 }
stud = students
students = { }
print(stud)
```

Output

{'Anil': 23, 'Sanjay': 28, 'Ajay': 25}

Tips

* By making a shallow copy, a new dictionary is not created. **stud** just starts pointing to the same data to which **students** was pointing.

* Had we used **students.clear( )** it would have cleared all the data, so students and stud both would have pointed to an empty dictionary.

Problem 9.2

Create a list of cricketers. Use this list to create a dictionary in which the list values become key values of the dictionary. Set the values of all keys to 50 in the dictionary created.

Program

```
lst = ['Sunil', 'Sachin', 'Rahul', 'Kapil', 'Sunil', 'Rahul']
d = dict.fromkeys(lst, 50)
print(len(lst))
print(len(d))
print(d)
```

Output

```
6
4
{'Sunil': 50, 'Sachin': 50, 'Rahul': 50, 'Kapil': 50}
```

Tips

* The list may contain duplicate items, whereas a dictionary always contains unique keys. Hence the dictionary is created from list, duplicates are eliminated, as seen in the output.

Problem 9.3

Create two lists students and marks. Create a dictionary from these two lists using dictionary comprehension. Use names as keys and marks as values.

Program

```
# lists of keys and values
lstnames = ['Sunil', 'Sachin', 'Rahul', 'Kapil', 'Rohit']
lstmarks = [54, 65, 45, 67, 78]
```

```
# dictionary comprehension
d = {k:v for (k, v) in zip(lstnames, lstmarks)}
print(d)
```

Output

{'Sunil': 54, 'Sachin': 65, 'Rahul': 45, 'Kapil': 67, 'Rohit': 78}

Problem 9.4

Write a program to sort a dictionary in ascending/descending order by key and ascending/descending order by value.

Program

```
import operator
d = {'Oil' : 230, 'Clip' : 150, 'Stud' : 175, 'Nut' : 35}
print('Original dictionary : ',d)

# sorting by key
d1 = sorted(d.items( ) )
print('Asc. order by key : ', d1)
d2 = sorted(d.items( ), reverse = True)
print('Des. order by key : ', d2)

# sorting by value
d1 = sorted(d.items( ), key = operator.itemgetter(1))
print('Asc. order by value : ', d1)
d2 = sorted(d.items( ), key = operator.itemgetter(1), reverse = True)
print('Des. order by value : ', d2)
```

Output

Original dictionary : {'Oil': 230, 'Clip': 150, 'Stud': 175, 'Nut': 35}
Asc. order by key : [('Clip', 150), ('Nut', 35), ('Oil', 230), ('Stud', 175)]
Des. order by key : [('Stud', 175), ('Oil', 230), ('Nut', 35), ('Clip', 150)]
Asc. order by value : [('Nut', 35), ('Clip', 150), ('Stud', 175), ('Oil', 230)]
Des. order by value : [('Oil', 230), ('Stud', 175), ('Clip', 150), ('Nut', 35)]

Tips

- By default items in a dictionary would be sorted as per the key.

- To sort by values we need to use **operator.itemgetter(1)**.

- The **key =** parameter of **sort( )** requires a key function (to be applied to be objects to be sorted) rather than a single key value.

- **operator.itemgetter(1)** will give you a function that grabs the first item from a list-like object.

- In general, **operator.itemgetter(n)** constructs a callable that assumes an iterable object (e.g. list, tuple, set) as input, and fetches the n-th element out of it.

Problem 9.5

Write a program to create three dictionaries and concatenate them to create fourth dictionary.

Program

```
d1 = {'Mango' : 30, 'Guava': 20}
d2 = {'Apple' : 70, 'Pineapple' : 50}
d3 = {'Kiwi' : 90, 'Banana' : 35}
d4 = { }
for d in (d1, d2, d3):
    d4.update(d)
print(d4)
```

Output

{'Mango': 30, 'Guava': 20, 'Apple': 70, 'Pineapple': 50, 'Kiwi': 90, 'Banana': 35}

Tips

- Lists are not efficient for implementation of queue data structure.

- With lists removal of items from beginning is not efficient, since it involves shifting of rest of the elements by 1 position after deletion.

- Hence for fast additions and deletions, **collections.dequeue** class is preferred.

Problem 9.6

Write a program to check whether a dictionary is empty or not.

Program

```
d1 = {'Anil' : 45, 'Amol' : 32}
if bool(d1) :
    print('Dictionary is not empty')

d2 = { }
if not bool(d2) :
    print('Dictionary is empty')
```

Output

```
Dictionary is not empty
Dictionary is empty
```

Problem 9.7

Create a dictionary containing names of students and marks obtained by them in three subjects. Write a program to print these names in tabular form with sorted names as columns and marks in three subjects listed below each student name as shown below.

Rahul	Rakesh	Sameer
67	59	58
76	70	86
39	81	78

Program

```
d = {'Rahul':[67,76,39],'Sameer':[58,86,78],'Rakesh':[59,70,81]}
for row in zip(*([k] + (v) for k, v in sorted(d.items( )))):
    print(*row, sep = '\t')
```

Problem 9.8

Suppose there are two dictionaries called boys and girls containing names as keys and ages as values. Write a program to merge the two dictionaries into a third dictionary.

Program

```
boys = {'Nilesh' : 41, 'Soumitra' : 42, 'Nadeem' : 47}
girls = {'Rasika' : 38, 'Rajashree': 43, 'Rasika' : 45}

combined = {**boys, **girls}
```

```
print(combined)

combined = {**girls, **boys}
print(combined)
```

Output

{'Nilesh': 41, 'Soumitra': 42, 'Nadeem': 47, 'Rasika': 45, 'Rajashree': 43}
{'Rasika': 45, 'Rajashree': 43, 'Nilesh': 41, 'Soumitra': 42, 'Nadeem': 47}

Tips

- From the output it can be observed that the dictionaries are merged in the order listed in the expression.

- As the merging takes place duplicates get overwritten from left to right. So Rasika : 38 got overwritten with Rasika : 45.

Problem 9.9

For the following dictionary, write a program to report the maximum salary.

Program

```
d = {
        'anuj' : {'salary' : 10000, 'age' : 20, 'height' : 6},
        'aditya' : {'salary' : 6000, 'age'  : 26, 'height' : 5.6},
        'rahul' : {'salary' : 7000, 'age'  : 26, 'height' : 5.9}
     }
lst = [ ]
for v in d.values( ) :
    lst.append(v['salary'])
print(max(lst))
print(min(lst))
```

Output

10000
6000

Problem 9.10

Suppose a dictionary contains roll numbers and names of students. Write a program to receive the roll number, extract the name corresponding to the roll number and display a message congratulating the student by his name. If the roll number doesn't exist in the dictionary the message should be 'Congratulations Student!'.

Program

```
students = { 554 : 'Ajay', 350: 'Ramesh', 395: 'Rakesh' }
rollno = int(input('Enter roll number: '))
name = students.get(rollno, 'Student')
print( f'Congratulations {name}!')
rollno = int(input('Enter roll number: '))
name = students.get(rollno, 'Student')
print( f'Congratulations {name}!')
```

Output

```
Enter roll number: 350
Congratulations Ramesh!
Enter roll number: 450
Congratulations Student!
```

 Exercise

[A] State whether the following statements are True or False:

(a) Dictionary elements can be accessed using position-based index.

(b) Dictionaries are immutable.

(c) **courses.clear( )** will delete the dictionary object called **courses**.

(d) It is possible to next dictionaries.

(e) It is possible to hold multiple values against a key in a dictionary.

[B] Attempt the following:

(a) Write a program that reads a string from the keyboard and creates dictionary containing frequency of each character occurring in the string. Also print these occurrences in the form of a histogram.

(b) Create a dictionary containing names of students and marks obtained by them in three subjects. Write a program to replace the marks in three subjects with the total in three in subjects, and average marks. Also report the topper of the class.

(c) Given the following dictionary:

portfolio = { 'accounts' : ['SBI', 'IOB']
              'shares' : ' [HDFC, 'ICICI', 'TM', 'TCS']
              'ornaments' : ['10 gm gold', '1 kg silver'] }

Write a program to perform the following operations:

- Add a key to portfolio called 'MF' with values 'Relaince' and 'ABSL'.
- Set the value of 'accounts' to be a list containing 'Axis' and 'BOB'.
- Sort the items in the list stored under the 'shares' key.
- Delete the list stored under 'ornaments' key.

(d) Create two dictionaries—one containing grocery items and their prices and another containing grocery item and quantity purchased. By using the values from these two dictionaries compute the total bill.

(e) Which functions will you use to fetch all keys, all values and key value pairs from a given dictionary?

(f) 36 unique combinations can result from use of two dice. Create a dictionary which stores these combinations as tuples.

(g) Create a dictionary of 10 user names and passwords. Receive the user name and password from keyboards and search for them in the dictionary. Print appropriate message on the screen based oon whether a match is found or not.

(h) A sparse matrix is a matrix most of whose elements have a value 0. Suppose we have a 5 x 5 sparse matrix stored as a list of lists. Write a program to create a dictionary from this list of lists. The dictionary should store the row and column of a non-zero element as a tuple key and the value of the non-zero element as the value against the key tuple.

(i) Given the following dictionary

marks= {'Subu' : {'Maths' : 88 , 'Eng' : 60, 'SSt' : 95},
        'Amol' : {'Maths' : 78 , 'Eng' : 68, 'SSt' : 89},
        'Rama' : {'Maths' : 68 , 'Eng' : 66, 'SSt' : 87},
        'Raka' : {'Maths' : 56 , 'Eng' : 66, 'SSt' : 77} }
Write a program to perform the following operations:

- Print marks obtained by Amol in English.

- Set marks obtained by Rama in Maths to 77.
- Sort the dictionary by name.

(j) Create a dictionary which stores the following data:

Interface	IP Address	status
eth0	1.1.1.1	up
eth1	2.2.2.2	up
wlan0	3.3.3.3	down
wlan1	4.4.4.4	up

Write a program to perform the following operations:

- Find the status of a given interface.
- Find interface and IP of all interfaces which are up.
- Find the total number of interfaces.
- Add two new entries to the dictionary.

10 Functions

- What are Functions?

- Communication with Functions

- Types of Arguments

- Unpacking Arguments

- Lambda Functions

- Recursive Functions

- Programs

- Exercise

What are Functions?

- Python function is a block of code that performs a specific and well-defined task.

- Two main advantages of function are:
    - (a) They help us divide our program into multiple tasks. For each task we can define a function. This makes the code modular.
    - (b) Functions provide a reuse mechanism.

- There are two types of Python functions:
    - (a) Built-in functions - Ex. len( ), sorted( ), min( ), max( ), etc.
    - (b) User-defined functions

- Given below is an example of user-defined function.

```
# function definition
def fun( ) :
    print('My opinions may have changed')
    print('But not the fact that I am right')
```

The body of the function must be indented suitably.

- A function can be called any number of times.

```
fun( )   # first call
fun( )   # second call
```

- When a function is called, control is transferred to the function, its statements are executed and control is returned to place from where the call originated.

- Python convention for function names:
    - Always use lowercase characters
    - Connect multiple words using _

Communication with Functions

- Communication with functions is done using parameters/arguments passed to it and the value(s) returned from it.

- The way to pass values to a function and return value from it is shown below:

```
def cal_sum(x, y, z) :
```

```
        return x + y + z

# pass 10, 20, 30 to cal_sum( ), collect value returned by it
s1 = cal_sum(10, 20, 30)
# pass a, b, c to cal_sum( ), collect value returned by it
a, b, c = 1, 2, 3
s2 = cal_sum(a, b, c)
```

- **return** statement returns control and value from a function. **return** without an expression returns **none**.

- To return multiple values from a function we can put them into a list/tuple/set/dictionary and then return it.

- Suppose we pass arguments **a, b, c** to a function and collect them in **x, y, z**. Changing **x, y, z** in the function body, changes **a, b, c**. Thus a function in Python is always called by reference.

Types of Arguments

- Arguments in a Python function can be of 4 types:

  (a) Required arguments or Positional arguments
  (b) Keyword arguments
  (c) Default arguments
  (d) Variable-length arguments

- Required argument must be passed in correct positional order. For example, if a function expects an int, float and string to be passed to it, then the call to this function should look like

  ```
  fun(10, 3.14, 'Rigmlarole') # correct call
  fun(3.14, 10, 'Rigmlarole') # incorrect order, won't work
  ```

  In required arguments number of arguments passed must match with number of arguments received.

- Keyword arguments can be passed out of order. Python interpreter uses keywords to match the values passed with the parameters used in the function definition.

  ```
  def print_it(i, a, str) :
      print(i, a, str)

  print_it(10, 3.14, 'Sicilian')   # ok
  print_it(a=3.14, i=10, str='Sicilian')   # ok
  ```

```
print_it(str='Sicilian', a=3.14, i=10)   # ok
print_it(str='Sicilian', i=10, a=3.14)   # ok
```

- Default arguments assume a default value, if we do not pass the value for that argument during the call.

```
def fun(a, b = 100, c = 3.14) :
    return a + b + c
```

```
x = fun(10)   # passes 10 to a, b is taken as 100, c as 3.14
y = fun(20, 50)  # passes 20, 50 to a, b. c is taken as 3.14
z = fun(30, 60, 6.28)   # passes 30, 60, 6.28 to a, b, c
```

- As the names suggests, variable-length arguments can be used in situations where the number of arguments is not fixed.

```
def print_it(*args) :
    print( )
    for var in args :
        print(var, end=' ')
```

```
print_it(10)   # ok
print_it(10, 3.14)   # ok
print_it(10, 3.14,'Sicilian')   # ok
print_it(10, 3.14, 'Sicilian', 'Punekar')   # ok
```

args used in definition of **print_it( )** is a tuple. * indicates that it will hold all the arguments passed to **print_it( )**.

- Before parameter representing variable number of arguments (args), 0 or more normal positional arguments may occur.

```
def print_it(i, a, s='Default string', *args) :
    print( )
    print(i, a, s, end=' ')
    for var in args :
        print(var, end=' ')
```

```
print_it(10, 3.14)
print_it(20, a=6.28)
print_it(a=6.28, i=30)
print_it(40, 2.35, 'Nagpur', 'Kolkattan')
```

- After args only keyword arguments can occur.

```
def fun(a, *args, s='!') :
    print(a, s)
    for i in args :
        print(i, s)

fun(10)
fun(10, 20)
fun(10, 20, 30)
fun(10, 20, 30, 40, s='+')
```

- It is possible to use all 4 types of arguments in a function.

Unpacking Arguments

- Suppose a function is expecting positional arguments and the arguments to be passed are in a list or tuple. In such a case we need to unpack the list or tuple using * operator before passing it to the function.

```
def print_it(a, b, c, d, e) :
    print(a, b, c, d, e)

lst = [10, 20, 30, 40, 50]
tpl = ('A', 'B', 'C', 'D', 'E')
print_it(*lst)
print_it(*tpl)
```

- Suppose a function is expecting keyword arguments and the arguments to be passed are in a dictionary. In such a case we need to unpack the dictionary using ** operator before passing it to the function.

```
def print_it(name='Sanjay', marks=75) :
    print(name, marks)

d = {'name' : 'Anil', 'marks' : 50}
print_it(*d)
print_it(**d)
```

The first call to print_it( ) passes keys to it, whereas, the second call passes values.

Lambda Functions

- Normal functions have names and they are defined using the **def** keyword. Anonymous functions do not have names and they are defined using the **lambda** keyword.

- An anonymous function defined using lambda can take any number of arguments but can return only one value.

  lambda arguments : expression

- Lambda functions can be used wherever function objects are required. Usually, it is used as an argument to other functions.

- Passing a lambda function:

  Suppose we wish to sort a dictionary by values using the **sorted( )** function. For this, we need to pass to **sorted( )** an anonymous function.

  ```
  d = {'Oil' : 230, 'Clip' : 150, 'Stud' : 175, 'Nut' : 35}
  # lambda takes a dictionary item and returns a value
  d1 = sorted(d.items( ), key = lambda kv : kv[1])
  print(d1)
  ```

  The sorted function uses a parameter key. This specifies a function of one argument that is used to extract a comparison for each element in the first argument of **sorted( )**. The default value of key is **None**, indicating that the elements in first argument are to be compared directly.

Recursive Functions

- A Python function can be called from within its body. When we do so it is called a recursive function.

  ```
  def fun( ) :
      # some statements
      if condition :
          fun( )    # recursive call
  ```

- Recursive call always leads to an infinite loop. So a provision must be made to get outside this infinite loop. The provision is done by making the recursive call either in the if block or in the else block.

- If recursive call is made in the if block, else block should contain the end condition logic. If recursive call is made in the else block, if block should contain the end condition logic.

- Fresh set of variables are born during each function call - normal call and recursive call.

- Variables die when control returns from a function.

- Recursive function may or may not have a return statement.

- Recursion is an alternative for a loop in logics that are expressible in the form of themselves.

- Understanding how a recursive function is working becomes easy if you make several copies of the same function on paper and then perform a dry run of the program.

p</>Programs

Problem 10.1

Write a program to receive three integers from keyboard and get their sum and product calculated through a user-defined function **cal_sum_prod( )**.

Program

```
def cal_sum_prod(x, y, z) :
    ss = x + y + z
    pp = x * y * z
    return ss, pp

a = int(input('Enter a: '))
b = int(input('Enter b: '))
c = int(input('Enter c: '))
s, p = cal_sum_prod(a, b, c)
print(s, p)
```

Output

```
Enter a: 10
Enter b: 20
Enter c: 30
```

60 6000

Tips

- Multiple values can be returned from a function as a tuple.

Problem 10.2

Pangram is a sentence that uses every letter of the alphabet. Write a program that checks whether a given string is pangram or not, through a user-defined function **ispangram( )**.

Program

```
def ispangram(s) :
    alphaset = set('abcdefghijklmnopqrstuvwxyz')
    return alphaset <= set(s.lower( ))

print ( ispangram('The quick brown fox jumps over the lazy dog'))
print ( ispangram('Crazy Fredrick bought many very exquisite opal
jewels'))
```

Tips

- **set( )** converts the string into a set of characters present in the string.

- <= checks whether **alphaset** is a subset of the given string.

Problem 10.3

Write a Python program that accepts a hyphen-separated sequence of words as input and call a function **convert( )** which converts it into a hyphen-separated sequence after sorting them alphabetically. For example, if the input string is

' here-come-the-dots-followed-by-dashes'

then, the converted string should be

'by-come-dashes-dots-followed-here-the'

Program

```
def convert(s1) :
    items = [s for s in s1.split('-')]
    items.sort( )
    s2 = '-'.join(items)
    return s2


s = 'here-come-the-dots-followed-by-dashes'
t = convert(s)
print(t)
```

Tips

- We have used list comprehension to create a list of words present in the string **s1**.

- The **join( )** method returns a string concatenated with the elements of an iterable. In our case the iterable is the list called **items**.

Problem 10.4

Write a Python function to create and return a list containing tuples of the form (x, x2, x3) for all x between 1 and 20 (both included).

Program

```
def generate_list( ):
    lst = list( )
    for i in range(1, 11):
        lst.append((i, i ** 2, i ** 3))

    return lst

l = generate_list( )
print(l)
```

Output

[(1, 1, 1), (2, 4, 8), (3, 9, 27), (4, 16, 64), (5, 25, 125), (6, 36, 216), (7, 49, 343), (8, 64, 512), (9, 81, 729), (10, 100, 1000)]

Tips

- **range(1, 11)** produces a list of numbers from 1 to 10.

- **append( )** adds a new tuple to the list in each iteration.

Problem 10.5

A palindrome is a word or phrase which reads the same in both directions. Given below are some palindromic strings:

deed
level
Malayalam
Rats live on no evil star
Murder for a jar of red rum

Write a program that defines a function **ispalindrome( )** which checks whether a given string is a palindrome or not. Ignore spaces while checking for palindrome.

Program

```
def ispalindrome(s):
    t = s.lower( )
    left = 0
    right = len(t) - 1

    while right >= left :
        if t[left] == ' ' :
            left += 1
        if t[right] == ' ' :
            right -= 1
        if t[left] != t[right]:
            return False
        left += 1
        right -= 1
    return True

print(ispalindrome('Malayalam'))
print(ispalindrome('Rats live on no evil star'))
print(ispalindrome('Murder for a jar of red rum'))
```

Output

True
True
True

Tips

- Since strings are immutable the string converted to lowercase has to be collected in another string **t**.

Problem 10.6

Write a program that defines a function **convert( )** that receives a string containing a sequence of whitespace separated words and returns a string after removing all duplicate words and sorting them alphanumerically.

For example, if the string passed to **convert( )** is

'Sakhi was a Hindu because her mother was a Hindu, and Sakhi's mother was a Hindu because her father was a Hindu

then, the output should be:

Hindu Hindu, Sakhi Sakhi's a and because father her mother was

Program

```
def convert(s) :
    words = [word for word in s.split(' ')]
    return ' '.join(sorted(list(set(words))))

s = 'I felt happy because I saw the others were happy and because I
knew I should feel happy, but I wasn\'t really happy'
t = convert(s)
print(t)

s = 'Sakhi was a Hindu because her mother was a Hindu, and Sakhi\'s
mother was a Hindu because her father was a Hindu'
t = convert(s)
print(t)
```

Output

I and because but feel felt happy happy, knew others really saw should the wasn't were
Hindu Hindu, Sakhi Sakhi's a and because father her mother was

Tips

- **set( )** removes duplicate data automatically.

- **list( )** converts the set into a list.

- **sorted( )** sorts the list data and returns sorted list.

- Sorted data list is converted to a string using **join( )**, appending a space at the end of each word, except the last.

Problem 10.7

Write a program that defines a function **count_alphabets_digits( )** that accepts a string and calculates the number of alphabets and digits in it. It should return these values as a dictionary. Call this function for some sample strings.

Program

```
def count_alphabets_digits(s) :
    d={'Digits' : 0, 'Alphabets' : 0}
    for ch in s:
        if ch.isalpha( ) :
            d['Alphabets'] += 1
        elif ch.isdigit( ) :
            d['Digits'] += 1
        else :
            pass
    return(d)

d = count_alphabets_digits('James Bond 007')
print(d)
d = count_alphabets_digits('Kholi Number 420')
print(d)
```

Output

{'Digits': 3, 'Alphabets': 9}

{'Digits': 3, 'Alphabets': 11}

Tips

- **pass** doesn't do anything on execution.

Problem 10.8

Write a program that defines a function **pascal_triangle( )** that displays a Pascal Triangle of level received as parameter to the function. A Pascal's Triangle of level 5 is shown below.

```
          1
        1   1
      1   2   1
    1   3   3   1
  1   4   6   4   1
```

Program

```
def pascal_triangle(n) :
    row = [1]
    z = [0]
    for x in range(n) :
        print(row)
        row = [l + r for l, r in zip(row + z, z + row)]

pascal_triangle(5)
```

Output

```
[1]
[1, 1]
[1, 2, 1]
[1, 3, 3, 1]
[1, 4, 6, 4, 1]
```

Tips

- For **n = 5**, **x** will vary from 0 to 4.

- **row + z** merges two lists.

- For x = 1, row=[1], z=[0], so,

  zip([1, 0], [0, 1]) gives tuples (1, 0), (0, 1)
  l + r gives row = [1, 1]

- For x = 2, row=[1, 1], z=[0], so,

  zip([1, 1, 0], [0, 1, 1]) gives tuples (1, 0), (1, 1), (0, 1)
  l + r gives [1, 2, 1]

- For x = 3, row=[1, 2, 1], z=[0], so,

  zip([1, 2, 1, 0], [0, 1, 2, 1]) gives tuples (1, 0), (2, 1), (1, 2), (0, 1)
  l + r gives [1, 3, 3, 1]

- For x = 4, row=[1, 3, 3, 1], z=[0], so,

  zip([1, 3, 3, 1, 0], [0, 1, 3, 3, 1]) gives (1, 0), (3, 1), (3, 3), (1, 3), (0, 1)
  l + r gives [1, 4, 6, 4, 1]

Problem 10.9

Following data shows names, ages and marks of students in a class:

Anil, 21, 80
Sohail, 20, 90
Sunil, 20, 91
Shobha, 18, 93
Anil, 19, 85

Write a program to sort this data on multiple keys in the order name, age and marks.

Program

```
import operator
lst = [('Anil', 21, 80), ('Sohail', 20, 90), ('Sunil', 20, 91),
        ('Shobha', 18, 93), ('Anil', 19, 85), ('Shobha', 20, 92)]
print(sorted(lst, key = operator.itemgetter(0, 1, 2)))
print(sorted(lst, key = lambda tpl : (tpl[0], tpl[1], tpl[2])))
```

Output

```
[('Anil', 19, 85), ('Anil', 21, 80), ('Shobha', 18, 93), ('Shobha', 20, 92),
('Sohail', 20, 90), ('Sunil', 20, 91)]
[('Anil', 19, 85), ('Anil', 21, 80), ('Shobha', 18, 93), ('Shobha', 20, 92),
('Sohail', 20, 90), ('Sunil', 20, 91)]
```

Tips

- Since there are multiple data items about a student, they have been put into a tuple.

- Since there are multiple students, all tuples have been put in a list.

- Two sorting methods have been used. In the first method **itemgetter( )** specifies the sorting order. In the second method a lambda has been used to specify the sorting order.

Problem 10.10

Write a program that defines a function called **frequency( )** which computes the frequency of words present in a string passed to it. The frequencies should be returned in sorted order by words in the string.

Program

```
def frequency ( s ) :
    freq = { }
    for word in s.split( ) :
        freq[word] = freq.get(word, 0) + 1
    return freq

sentence = 'It is true for all that that that that \
that that that refers to is not the same that \
that that that refers to'
d = frequency(sentence)
words = sorted(d)

for w in words:
    print ('%s:%d' % (w, d[w]))
```

Output

```
It:1
all:1
for:1
is:2
not:1
refers:2
same:1
that:11
```

the:1
to:2
true:1

Tips

- We did not use **freq[word] = freq[word] + 1** because we have not initialized all word counts for each unique word to 0 to begin with.

- When we use **freq.get(word, 0)**, **get( )** searches the word. If it is not found, the second parameter, i.e. 0 will be returned. Thus, for first call for each unique word, the word count is properly initialized to 0.

- **sorted( )** returns a sorted list of key values in the dictionary.

- **w. d[w]** yields the word and its frequency count stored in the dictionary **d**.

Problem 10.11

Write a program that defines two functions called **create_sent1( )** and **create_sent2( )**. Both receive following 3 lists:

subjects = ['He', 'She']
verbs = ['loves', 'hates']
objects = ['TV Serials','Netflix']

Both functions should form sentences by picking elements from these lists and return them. Use **for** loops in **create_sent1( )** and list comprehension in **create_sent2( )**.

Program

```
def create_sent1(sub, ver, obj) :
    lst = [ ]
    for i in range(len(sub)) :
        for j in range(len(ver)) :
            for k in range(len(obj)) :
                sent = sub[i] + ' ' + ver[j] + ' ' + obj[k]
                lst.append(sent)
    return lst

def create_sent2(sub, ver, obj) :
    return [(s + ' ' + v + ' ' + o) for s in sub for v in ver for o in obj]
```

```
subjects = ['He', 'She']
verbs = ['loves', 'hates']
objects = ['TV Serials','Netflix']

lst1 = create_sent1( subjects, verbs, objects)
for l in lst1 :
    print(l)

print( )
lst2 = create_sent2( subjects, verbs, objects)
for l in lst2 :
    print(l)
```

Output

He loves TV Serials
He loves Netflix
He hates TV Serials
He hates Netflix
She loves TV Serials
She loves Netflix
She hates TV Serials
She hates Netflix

He loves TV Serials
He loves Netflix
He hates TV Serials
He hates Netflix
She loves TV Serials
She loves Netflix
She hates TV Serials
She hates Netflix

 Exercise

[A] Answer the following:

(a) Write a program that defines a function **count_lower_upper( )** that accepts a string and calculates the number of uppercase and lowercase alphabets in it. It should return these values as a dictionary. Call this function for some sample strings.

(b) Write a program that defines a function **compute( )** that calculates the value of n + nn + nnn + nnnn, where n is digit received by the function. Test the function for digits 4 and 7.

(c) Write a program that defines a function **create_array( )** to create and return a 3D array whose dimensions are passed to the function. Also initialize each element of this array to a value passed to the function.

(d) Write a program that defines a function **create_list( )** to create and return a list which is an intersection of two lists passed to it.

(e) Write a program that defines a function **sanitize_list( )** to remove all duplicate entries from the list that it receives.

(a) A 5-digit positive integer is entered through the keyboard, write a recursive function to calculate sum of digits of the 5-digit number.

(f) A positive integer is entered through the keyboard; define a recursive function that obtains the prime factors of the number.

(g) Define a recursive function to obtain the first 25 numbers of a Fibonacci sequence. In a Fibonacci sequence the sum of two successive terms gives the third term. Following are the first few terms of the Fibonacci sequence:

1 1 2 3 5 8 13 21 34 55 89...

(h) Define a recursive function to obtain the sum of first 25 natural numbers.

11 Modules and Packages

- The Main Module
- Multiple Modules
- Symbol Table
- *vars( )* and *dir( )* Functions
- Variations of import
- Same Code, Different Interpretation
- Search Sequence
- Globals and Locals
- *global( )* and *local( )*
- Packages
- Programs
- Exercise

The Main Module

- A module is a .py file containing definitions and statements. So all .py files that we created for our programs are modules.

- When we execute a program its module name is **__main__**. This name is available in the variable **__name__**.

```
def display( ) :
    print('You cannot make History if you use Incognito Mode')

def show( ) :
    print('Pizza is a pie chart of how much pizza is left')

print(__name__)
display( )
show( )
```

On execution of this program, we get the following output:

```
__main__
You cannot make History if you use Incognito Mode
Pizza is a pie chart of how much pizza is left
```

Multiple Modules

- There are two reasons why we may want to create a program that contains multiple modules:

  (a) It makes sense to split a big program into multiple .py files, where each .py file acts as a module.

  Benefit - Ease of development and maintenance.

  (b) You may need a set of handy functions in several programs. In such a case instead of copying these functions in different program files, we may keep them in one file and used them in different programs.

  Benefit - Reuse of existing code

- To use the definition and statements in a module in another module, we need to 'import' it into current module.

```
# functions.py
def display( ) :
    print('Earlier rich owned cars, while poor had horses')

def show( ) :
    print('Now everyone has car, while only rich own horses')


# usefunctions.py
import functions
functions.display( )
functions.show( )
```

- When we execute 'usefunctions.py', it runs as a module with name **__main__**.

- **import functions** makes the definitions in 'functions.py' available in 'usefunctions.py'.

- A module can import multiple modules.

```
import math
import random
import functions

a = 100
b = 200
print(__name__)
print(math.sin(0.5))
print(random.randint(30, 45))
functions.display( )
functions.show( )
```

Here **__name__** contains **__main__** indicating that we are executing the main module. **random** and **math** are standard modules. **functions** is a user-defined module.

Symbol Table

- While interpreting our program Python interpreter creates a symbol table.

- This table consists of relevant information about each identifier used in our program. This includes the type of the identifier, its scope level and its location.

- This table is referred by the interpreter to decide whether the operations performed by our program on the identifiers should be permitted or not.

- For example, if we have an identifier whose type has been marked as tuple in the symbol table. Later in the program if we try to modify its contents interpreter will report an error as a tuple is immutable.

vars( ) and *dir( )* Functions

- There are two useful global functions **vars( )** and **dir( )**. Of these, **vars( )** returns a dictionary, whereas **dir( )** returns a list. They can be used in this form:

```
vars( )
vars(module/class/object)
dir( )
dir(module/class/object)
```

Given below is the sample usage of these functions:

```
import math
import functions
a = 125
s = 'Spooked'

# prints dict of names in the current module including a and s
print(vars( ))
print(vars(math))        # prints dict of names in math module
print(vars(functions))   # prints dict of names in functions module

# prints list of attributes in current module including a and s
print(dir( ))
print(dir(math))         # prints list of attributes in math module
print(dir(functions))    # prints list of attributes in functions module
```

Variations of *import*

- The **import** statement can be used in multiple forms.

```
import math
import random
is same as

import maths, random
```

- If we wish, we can import specific names from a module.

  from maths import sin, cos, tan
  from functions import display
  from myfunctions import *

- We can rename a module while importing it. We can then use the new name in place of the original module name.

  import functions as fun
  fun.display( )

  or even

  from functions import display as disp
  disp( )

Same Code, Different Interpretation

- Suppose we have a module called **functions** in 'functions.py'. If this module has functions **display( )** and **main( )**. We want to use this program sometime as an independent script, and at other times as a module from which we can use **display( )** function.

- To achieve this, we need to write the code in this fashion:

```
# functions.py
def display( ) :
    print('Wright Brothers are responsible for 9/11 too')

def main( ) :
    print('If you beat your own record, you win as well as lose')
    print('Internet connects people at a long distance')
    print('Internet disconnects people at a short distance')
    display( )

if ( __name__ == '__main__') :
    main( )
```

If we run it as an independent program, **if** will be satisfied. As a result, **main( )** will be called. The name of this function need not be **main( )**.

If we import this module in another program, **if** will fail, so **main( )** will not be called. The program can call **display( )** independently.

Search Sequence

- If we import a module called 'myfuncs', following search sequence will be followed:

- Interpreter will first search for a built-in module called 'myfuncs'.

- If such a module is not found, then it will search for it in directory list given by the variable **sys.path**.

- The list in the **sys.path** variable contains directory from where the script has been executed, followed by a list of directory as specified in **PYTHONPATH** environment variable.

- If we want, we can modify the **sys.path** variable.

- We can print the list of directories in **sys.path** using:

```
for p in sys.path
    print(p)
```

Globals and Locals

- We propose to learn objects in detail in Chapter 12. As of now, it will suffice to say that an object is a nameless entity containing data and methods.

- Methods are nothing but functions defined in an object. Methods work with object's data.

- Variables that we create are identifiers that refer to an object. For example, in **a = 20**, 20 is stored in a nameless object. Address of this nameless object is stored in the identifier **a**.

- A namespace is a dictionary of identifiers (keys) and their corresponding objects (values).

- An identifier used in a function or a method belongs to the **local namespace**.

- An identifier used outside a function or a method belongs to the **global namespace**.

- If a local and a global identifier have the same name, the local identifier shadows out the global identifier.

- Python assumes that an identifier that is assigned a value in a function/method is a local identifier.

- If we wish to assign a value to a global identifier within a function/method, we should explicitly declare the variable as global using the **global** keyword.

```
def fun( ) :
    # name conflict. local a shadows out global a
    a = 45

    # name conflict, use global b
    global b
    b = 6.28

    # uses local a, global b and s
    # no need to define s as global, since it is not being changed
    print(a, b, s)

# global identifiers
a = 20
b = 3.14
s = 'Aabra Ka Daabra'
lst = [10, 20, 30, 40, 50]
fun( )
```

global( ) and *local( )*

- List of identifiers in global and local namespaces van be obtained using built-in functions **globals( )** and **locals( )**.

- If **locals( )** is called from within a function/method, it returns a dictionary of identifiers that are accessible from that function/method.

- If **globals( )** is called from within a function/method, it returns a dictionary of global identifiers that can be accessed from that function/method.

```
def fun( ) :
    a = 45
    global b
    b = 6.28
```

```
    print(locals( ))
    print(globals( ))

a = 20
b = 3.14
s = 'Aabra Ka Daabra'
fun( )
```

On execution of this program, we get the following output:

```
{'a': 45}
{'a': 20, 'b': 6.28, 's': 'Aabra Ka Daabra'}
```

The second line above shows abridged output.

Packages

- The way drives, folders, subfolders help us organize files in an OS, packages help us organize sub-packages and modules.

- A particular directory is treated as a package if it contains a file named __init__.py in it. The directory may contain other sub-packages and modules in it. __init__.py file may be empty or it may contain some initialization code for the package.

- Suppose there is a package called **pkg** containing a module called **mod.py**. If the module contains functions **f1( )** and **f2( )** then the directory structure and the program to use **f1( )** and **f2( )** would be as follows:

```
Directory - pkg
Contents of pkg directory - mod.py and __init__.py
Contents of mod.py - f1( ) and f2( )
Program to use f1( ) and f2( )
# mod.py
def f1( ) :
print('Inside function f1')
def f2( ) :
print('Inside function f2')

# client.py
import pkg.mod
mod.f1( )
mod.f2( )
```

Problem 11.1

Write a program to get a list of built-in functions.

Program

```
import builtins
print(dir(builtins))
```

Output

```
Enter a: 10
Enter b: 20
Enter c: 30
60 6000
```

Tips

- Multiple values can be returned from a function as a tuple.

Problem 11.2

Suppose we have defined two functions **msg1( )** and **msg2( )** in main module. What will be the output of **vars( )** and **dir( )** on the current module? How will you obtain the list of names which are present in both outputs, those which are unique to either list?

Program

```
def msg1( ) :
    print('Wright Brothers are responsible for 9/11 too')
def msg2( ) :
    print('Cells divide to multiply')
d = vars( )
l = dir( )
print(sorted(d.keys()))
print(l)
print(d.keys( ) - l)
print(l - d.keys( ))
```

Output

```
['__annotations__', '__builtins__', '__cached__', '__doc__', '__file__',
'__loader__', '__name__', '__package__', '__spec__', 'd', 'l', 'msg1',
'msg2']
['__annotations__', '__builtins__', '__cached__', '__doc__', '__file__',
'__loader__', '__name__', '__package__', '__spec__', 'd', 'msg1', 'msg2']
{'l'}
set( )
```

Tips

- **set( )** means an empty set. It means there is nothing in **l** that is not present in **d**.

Problem 11.3

Write a Python program that is organized as follows:

Packages:
messages.funny
messages.curt

Modules:
modf1.py, modf2.py, modf3.py in package messages.funny
modc1.py, modc2.py, modc3.py in package messages.curt

Functions:
funf1( ) in module modf1
funf1( ) in module modf1
funf1( ) in module modf1
funf1( ) in module modf1
funf1( ) in module modf1
funf1( ) in module modf1

Use all the functions in a program **client.py**.

Program

Directory structure will be as follows:

messages
    __init__.py
   funny
       __init__.py
      modf1.py

```
        modf2.py
        modf3.py
    curt
        __init__.py
        modc1.py
        modc2.py
        modc3.py
client.py
```

Of these, **messages, funny** and **curt** are directories, rest are files. All **__init__.py** are empty files.

```
# modf1.py
def funf1( ) :
    print('The ability to speak several languages is an asset...')
    print('ability to keep your mouth shut in any language is priceless')
```

```
# modf2.py
def funf2( ) :
    print('If you cut off your left arm...')
    print('then your right arm would be left')
```

```
# modf3.py
def funf3( ) :
    print('Alcohol is a solution!')
```

```
# modc1.py
def func1( ) :
  print('The ability to speak several languages is an asset...')
  print('but the ability to keep your mouth shut in any language is
priceless'
# modc2.py
def func2( ) :
  print('There is no physical evidence to say that today is Tuesday...')
  print('We have to trust someone who kept the count since first day')
```

```
# modc3.py
def func3( ) :
  print('We spend five days a week pretending to be someone else...')
  print('in order to spend two days being who we are')
```

```
# client.py
import messages.funny.modf1
import messages.funny.modf2
import messages.funny.modf3

import messages.curt.modc1
import messages.curt.modc2
import messages.curt.modc3

messages.funny.modf1.funf1( )
messages.funny.modf2.funf2( )
messages.funny.modf3.funf3( )

messages.curt.modc1.func1( )
messages.curt.modc2.func2( )
messages.curt.modc3.func3( )
```

Tips

- Directory structure is very important. For a directory to qualify as a package, it has to contain a file **__init__.py**.

Problem 11.4

Rewrite the import statements in Program 11.3, such that using functions in different modules becomes convenient.

Program

```
from messages.curt.modc1 import func1
from messages.curt.modc2 import func2
from messages.curt.modc3 import func3

from messages.funny.modf1 import funf1
from messages.funny.modf2 import funf2
from messages.funny.modf3 import funf3

funf1( )
funf2( )
funf3( )

func1( )
func2( )
```

func3( )

Tips

- Benefit - Calls to functions does not need the dotted syntax.

- Limitation - Only the specified function gets imported.

Problem 11.5

Can we rewrite the following imports using * notation?

from messages.curt.modc1 import func1
from messages.curt.modc2 import func2
from messages.curt.modc3 import func3

from messages.funny.modf1 import funf1
from messages.funny.modf2 import funf2
from messages.funny.modf3 import funf3

Program

We may use the following import statements:

```
# client.py
from messages.curt.modc1 import *
from messages.curt.modc2 import *
from messages.curt.modc3 import *

from messages.funny.modf1 import *
from messages.funny.modf2 import *
from messages.funny.modf3 import *

funf1( )
funf2( )
funf3( )

func1( )
func2( )
func3( )
```

Tips

- Limitation - Since there is only one function in each module, using * is not so useful.

- Also, * is not so popular as it does not indicate which function/class are we importing.

 **Exercise**

[A] Answer the following:

(a) Suppose there are three modules **m1.py**, **m2.py**, **m3.py**, containing functions **f1( )**, **f2( )** and **f3( )** respectively. How will you use those functions in your program?

(b) Write a program containing functions **fun1( )**, **fun2( )**, **fun3( )** and some statements. Add suitable code to the program such that you can use it as a module or a normal program.

(c) Suppose a module **mod.py** contains functions **f1( )**, **f2( )** and **f3( )**. Write 4 forms of import statements to use these functions in your program.

[B] Attempt the following:

(a) What is the purpose behind creating multiple packages and modules?

(b) By default, to which module do the statements in a program belong? How do we access the name of this module?

(c) In the following statement what do **a, b, c, x** represent?

import a.b.c.x

(d) If module **m** contains a function **fun( )**, what is wrong with the following statements?

import m
fun( )

(e) What is the purpose of built-in functions **dir( )**, **vars( )**, **global( )** and **local( )**?

(f) What are the contents of **PYTHONPATH** variable? How can we access its contents programmatically?

(g) What does the content of **sys.path** signify? What does the order of contents of **sys.path** signify?

(h) What will be the output of the following program?

```
var = 1.1
print(var)

def fun( ) :
    var = 2.2
    print(var)

fun( )
print(var)
```

(i) Do the following import statements serve the same purpose?

```
# version 1
import a, b, c

# version 2
import a
import b
import c

# version 3
from a import *
from b import *
from c import *
```

[C] State whether the following statements are True or False:

(a) A variable with same name may be present in local namespace as well as the global namespace.

(b) A function can belong to a module and the module can belong to a package.

(c) A package can contain one or more modules in it.

(d) Nested packages are allowed.

(e) Contents of **sys.path** variable cannot be modified.

(f) In the statement **import a.b.c**, **c** cannot be a function.

(g) It is a good idea to use * to import all the funtions/classes defined in a module.

[D] Match the following:

dir( )	Nested packages
vars( )	Identifiers, their type and scope
Variables in a function	Returns dictionary
import a.b.c	Local namespace
Symbol table	Returns list
Variables outside all functions	Global namespace

12

Classes and Objects

- Programming Paradigms

- Public and Private Members

- Class Declaration and Object Creation

- Class Variables and Methods

- Object and Class Attributes

- Programs

- Exercise

Programming Paradigms

- Paradigm means the principle according to which a program is organized to carry out a given task.

- Structured programming paradigm encourages breaking down a given task into smaller tasks, writing function for each task and carrying out interaction of these functions.

- Object-oriented programming paradigm encourages creation and interaction of objects.

- Python supports structured as well as object-oriented programming paradigms.

What are Classes and Objects?

- A class contains data and methods that can access or manipulate this data. Thus a class lets us bundle data and functionality together.

- A class is generic in nature, whereas an object is specific in nature.

- Examples of classes and objects:

  Bird is a class. Sparrow, Crow, Eagle are objects of Bird class.
  Player is a class. Sachin, Rahul, Kapil are objects of Player class.
  Flower is a class. Rose, Lily, Jarbera are objects of Flower class.
  Instrument is a class. Sitar, Flute are objects of Instrument lass.

- Programmatic examples of classes and objects:

  ```
  i = 10              # i is an object of int class
  a = 3.14            # a is an object of float class
  s = 'Sudesh'        # s is an object of str class
  lst = [ 10, 20, 30] # lst is an object of list class
  tpl = ('a', 'b', 'c')   # tpl is an object of tuple class
  ```

  int, float, str, list, tuple are ready-made classes.

- Apart from using Python library's ready-made classes, we can also create our own classes. These are often called user-defined data types.

- A user-defined class **Employee** may contain data like **name, age, salary** and methods like **print_data( )** and **set_data( )** to access and manipulate the data.

- Objects created from **Employee** class will have specific values for data. Hence, each object is a specific instance of a class. Creation of an object is often called instantiation.

- The specific data in an object is often called **instance data** or **state** of the object or **attributes** of the object.

Public and Private Members

- Members of a class (data and methods) are accessible from outside the class.

- It is a good idea to keep data in a class inaccessible from outside the class and access it through member functions of the class.

- Private members by convention start with an underscore, as in **_name, _age, _salary**.

Class Declaration and Object Creation

```
class Employee :
    def set_data(self, n, a, s) :
        self._name = n
        self._age = a
        self._salary = s

    def display_data(self) :
        print(self._name, self._age, self._salary)

e1 = Employee( )
e1.set_data('Ramesh', 23, 25000)
e1.display_data( )
e2 = Employee( )
e2.set_data('Suresh', 25, 30000)
e2.display_data( )
```

- Here we have defined a **Employee** class with 3 private data members **_name, _age, _salary** and two public methods **set_data( )** and **display_data( )**.

- **e1 = Employee( )** creates a nameless object and stores its address in **e1**.

- Methods of a class can be called using the syntax **object.method( )**.

- Whenever we call a method using an object, address of the object gets passed to the method implicitly. This address is collected by the method in a variable called **self**.

- **self** is like **this** pointer of C++ or **this** reference of Java. In place of **self** any other variable name can be used.

- **e1.set_data('Ramesh', 23, 25000)** calls the method **set_data( )**. First parameter passed to this method is the address of object, followed by name, age and salary.

- When **set_data( )** is called using **e1**, **self** contains the address of first object. Likewise, when **set_data( )** is called using **e2**, **self** contains address of the second object.

- Data in class **Employee**, i.e. **_name, _age, _salary** is called instance data, whereas methods **set_data( )** and **display_data( )** are called instance methods.

- In principle, every object has instance data and instance methods.

- In practice, each object has instance data, whereas methods are shared amongst objects.

- Sharing is justified, as from one object to another, methods are going to remain same.

Object Initialization

```
class Employee :
    def set_data(self, n, a, s) :
        self._name = n
        self._age = a
        self._salary = s

    def display_data(self) :
        print(self._name, self._age, self._salary)

    def __init__(self, n = ' ', a = 0, s = 0.0) :
        self._name = n
```

```
        self._age = a
        self._salary = s

    def __del__(self) :
        print('Deleting object' + str(self))

e1 = Employee('Ramesh', 23, 25000)
e1.display_data( )
e2 = Employee( )
e2.set_data('Suresh', 25, 30000)
e2.display_data( )
```

On execution of this program, we get the following output:

Ramesh 23 25000
Suresh 25 30000
Deleting object<__main__.Employee object at 0x013F6810>
Deleting object<__main__.Employee object at 0x013F65B0>

- There are two ways to initialize an object :

  Method 1 : Using methods like **get_data( ) / set_data( )**

  Benefit - Data is protected from manipulation from outside the class.

  Method 2 : Using special member function **__init__( )**

  Benefit - Guaranteed initialization, as **__init__( )** is always called
  when an object is created.

- **__init__( )** is similar to constructor function of C++ / Java.

- When an object is created, space is allocated in memory and **__init__( )** is called. So address of object is passed to **__init__( )**.

- **__init__( )** doesn't return any value.

- **__init__( )** is called only once during entire lifetime of an object.

- If we do not define **__init__( )**, then Python provides a default **__init__( )** method.

- A class may have **__init__( )** as well as **set_data( )**.

  __init__( ) – To initialize object
  set_data( ) – To modify object

- **__init__( )**'s parameters can take default values. In our program they get used while creating object **e2**.

- __del__( ) method gets called automatically when an object goes out of scope. Cleanup activity, if any, should be done in __del__( ).

- __del__( ) is similar to destructor function of C++.

Class Variables and Methods

- If we wish to share a variable amongst all objects of a class, we must declare the variable as a **class variable** or a **class attribute**.

- To declare a class variable, we have to create a variable without prepending it with **self**.

- Class variables do not become part of objects of a class.

- Class variables are accessed using the syntax **classname.varname**.

- Contrasted with instance methods, **class methods** are methods that do not receive a **self** argument.

- Class methods can be accessed using the syntax **classname.methodname( )**.

- Class variables can be used to count how many objects have been created from a class.

- Class variables and methods are like static members in C++ / Java.

Accessing Object and Class Attributes

```
class Fruit :
    count = 0

    def __init__(self, name = ' ', size = 0, color = ' ') :
        self._name = name
        self._size = size
        self._color = color
        Fruit.count += 1

    def display( ) :
        print(Fruit.count)

f1 = Fruit('Banana', 5, 'Yellow')
print(vars(f1))
print(dir(f1))
```

On execution of this program, we get the following output:

{'_Fruit__name': 'Banana', '_Fruit__size': 5, '_Fruit__color': 'Yellow'}

['__class__', '__delattr__', '__dict__', '__dir__', '__doc__', '__eq__', '__format__', '__ge__', '__getattribute__', '__gt__', '__hash__', '__init__', '__init_subclass__', '__le__', '__lt__', '__module__', '__ne__', '__new__', '__reduce__', '__reduce_ex__', '__repr__', '__setattr__', '__sizeof__', '__str__', '__subclasshook__', '__weakref__', '_Fruit__color', '_Fruit__name', '_Fruit__size', 'count', 'display']

- A specific object's attributes can be obtained using the **vars( )** built-in function. They are returned as a dictionary.

- A class's attributes can be obtained using the **dir( )** built-in function. They are returned as a list.

Problem 12.1

Write a program to create a class called **Fruit** with attributes **size** and **color**. Create multiple objects of this class. Report how many objects have been created from the class.

Program

```
class Fruit :
    count = 0

    def __init__(self, name = ' ', size = 0, color = ' ') :
        self._name = name
        self._size = size
        self._color = color
        Fruit.count += 1

    def display( ) :
        print(Fruit.count)

f1 = Fruit('Banana', 5, 'Yellow')
f2 = Fruit('Orange', 4, 'Orange')
f3 = Fruit('Apple', 3, 'Red')
Fruit.display( )
```

```
print(Fruit.count)
```

Output

```
3
3
```

Tips

- **count** is a class attribute, not an object attribute. So it is shared amongst all Fruit objects.

- It can be initialized as **count = 0**, but must be accessed using **Fruit.count**.

Problem 12.2

Write a program that determines whether two objects are of same type, whether their attributes are same and whether they are pointing to same object.

Program

```
class Complex :
    def __init__(self, r = 0.0, i = 0.0) :
        self._real = r
        self._imag = i

    def __eq__(self, other ) :
        if self._real == other._real and self._imag == other._imag :
            return True
        else :
            return False

c1 = Complex(1.1, 0.2)
c2 = Complex(2.1, 0.4)
c3 = c1
if c1 == c2 :
    print('Attributes of c1 and c2 are same')
else :
    print('Attributes of c1 and c2 are different')

if type(c1) == type(c3) :
```

```
        print('c1 and c3 are of same type')
else :
        print('c1 and c3 are of different type' )

if c1 is c3 :
        print('c1 and c3 are pointing to same object')
else :
        print('c1 and c3 are pointing to different objects' )
```

Output

Attributes of c1 and c2 are different
c1 and c3 are of same type
c1 and c3 are pointing to same object

Tips

- To compare attributes of two **Complex** objects we have overloaded the == operator, by defining the function **__eq__( )**. Operator overloading is explained in detail in Chapter 13.

- **type( )** is used to obtain the type of an object. Types can be compared using the == operator.

- **is** keyword is used to check whether **c1** and **c3** are pointing to the same object.

Problem 12.3

Write a Python program that displays the attributes of integer, float and function objects. Also show how these attributes can be used.

Program

```
def fun( ) :
        print('Everything is an object')

print(dir(55))
print(dir(-5.67))
print(dir(fun))
print((5).__add__(6))
print((-5.67).__abs__( ))
d = globals()
d['fun'].__call__( )
```

Output

```
['__abs__', '__add__', '__and__', '__bool__', '__ceil__', ...]
['__abs__', '__add__', '__bool__', '__class__', '__delattr__', ...]
['__annotations__', '__call__', '__class__', '__closure__', ... ]
11
5.67
Everything is an object
```

Tips

- Output shows incomplete list of attributes of **int, float** and **function** objects.

- From this list we have used the attributes **__add__**( ) to add two integers, **__abs__**( ) to get absolute value of float and **__call__**( ) to call the function **fun( )**.

- **globals( )** return a dictionary representing the current global symbol table. From this dictionary we have picked the object representing the **fun** function and used it to call **__call__**( ). This results into call to **fun( )**.

 **Exercise**

[A] State whether the following statements are True or False:

(a) Class attributes and object attributes are same.

(b) A class data member is useful when all objects of the same class must share a common item of information.

(c) If a class has a data member and three objects are created from this class, then each object would have its own data member.

(d) A class can have class data as well as class functions.

(e) Usually data in a class is kept private and the data is accessed / manipulated through public member functions of the class.

(f) Member functions of a class have to be called explicitly, whereas, the constructor gets called automatically.

(g) A constructor gets called whenever an object gets instantiated.

(h) A constructor never returns a value.

(i) When an object goes out of scope, its destructor gets called automatically.

(j) The **self** variable always contains the address of the object using which the method/data is being accessed.

(k) The **self** variable can be used even outside the class.

(l) A constructor gets called only during the lifetime of an object.

(m) By default, instance data and methods in a class are public.

(n) In a class 2 constructors can exist—a 0-rgument constructor and 2-argument constructor can exist.

[B] Answer the following:

(a) Which methods in a class act as constructor and destructor?

(b) What is the difference between the function **vars( )** and **dir( )**?

(c) How many object are created in the following code snippet?

```
a = 10 ; b = a ;
c = b
```

(d) What is the difference between variables, **age** and **_age**?

[C] Attempt the following:

(a) Write a program to create a class that represents Complex numbers containing real and imaginary parts and then use it to perform complex number addition, subtraction, multiplication and division.

(b) Write a program that implements a **Matrix** class and performs addition, multiplication, and transpose operations on 3 x 3 matrices.

(c) Write a program to create a class that can calculate the surface area and volume of a solid. The class should also have a provision to accept the data relevant to the solid.

(d) Write a program to create a class that can calculate the perimeter / circumference and area of a regular shape. The class should also have a provision to accept the data relevant to the shape.

(e) Write a program that creates and uses a **Time** class to perform various time arithmetic operations.

Intricacies of
Classes & Objects

Identifier Naming Convention

- We have created identifiers for many things—normal variable, functions, classes, instance data, instance methods, class data and class methods.

- It is a good idea to follow the following convention while creating identifiers:

  (a) Class names - Start with an uppercase letter.
      Ex. : Employee, Fruit, Bird, Complex, Tool, Machine

  (b) All other identifiers - Start with a lowercase letter.
      Ex. real, imag, name, age, salary, printit( ), display( )

  (c) Private identifiers - Start with a single leading underscore.
      Ex. _name, _age, _set_data( ), _get_errors( )

      Python does not have keywords private or public to mark the attributes as private/public. So by convention an attribute/method beginning with an underscore indicates that you shouldn't access it from outside the class.

  (d) Strongly private identifier - Start with two leading underscores (often called dunderscore, short for double underscore).
      Ex. __set_data( ), __get_data( )

      Such names have relevance in a OO concept called Inheritance (discussed in Chapter 13). When you create a method starting with __ you're saying that you don't want anybody to override it, it will be accessible just from inside its own class.

  (e) Language-defined special names - Start and end with two __.
      Ex. __init__( ), __del__( ), __add__( ), __sub__( )

      Don't call these methods. They are the methods that Python calls.

  (f) Keywords - Do not use them as identifier names.

Calling Functions and Methods

```
def printit( ) :
    print('Opener')
```

```
class Message :
    def display(self, msg) :
        printit( )
        print(msg)

    def show( ) :
        printit( )
        print('Hello')
        # display( )   # this call will result in an error

m = Message( )
m.display('Good Morning' )
Message.show( )
```

On execution of this program, we get the following output:

```
Opener
Good Morning
Opener
Hello
```

- Class method **show( )** does not receive **self**, whereas instance method **display( )** does.

- A global function **printit( )** can call a class method **show( )** and instance method **display( )**.

- A class method and instance method can call a global function **printit( )**.

- A class method **show( )** cannot call an object method **display( )** since **show( )** doesn't receive a **self** argument. In absence of this argument **display( )** will not know which object is it supposed to work with.

- If **prinit( )** so desires, it can call the class method as well as instance method.

- A class method and instance method can also be called from a method of another class. The syntax for doing so remains same:

```
m2 = Message( )
m2.display('Good Afternoon')
Message.show( 'Hi' )
```

Operator Overloading

```
class Complex :
    def __init__(self, r = 0.0, i = 0.0) :
        self._real = r
        self._imag = i

    def __add__(self, other ) :
        z = Complex( )
        z._real = self._real + other._real
        z._imag = self._imag + other._imag
        return z

    def __sub__(self, other ) :
        z = Complex( )
        z._real = self._real - other._real
        z._imag = self._imag - other._imag
        return z

    def display(self) :
        print(self._real, self._imag)

c1 = Complex(1.1, 0.2)
c2 = Complex(1.1, 0.2)
c3 = c1 + c2
c3.display( )
c4 = c1 - c2
c4.display( )
```

- Since **Complex** is a user-defined class, Python doesn't know how to add objects of this class. We can teach it how to do it, by overloading the + operator.

- To overload the + operator we need to define **__add__( )** function within the **Complex** class.

- Likewise, to overload the - operator we need define **__sub__( )** function for carrying out subtraction of two **Complex** objects.

- In the expression **c3 = c1 + c2**, **c1** becomes available in **self**, whereas, **c2** is collected in **other**.

- Given below is the list of operators that we can overload and their function equivalents that we need to define.

```
# Arithmetic operators
+          __add__(self, other)
-          __sub__(self, other)
*          __mul__(self, other)
/          __truediv__(self, other)
%          __mod__(self, other)
**         __pow__(self, other)
//         __floordiv__(self, other)


# Comparison operators
<          __lt__(self, other)
>          __gt__(self, other)
<=         __le__(self, other)
>=         __ge__(self, other)
==         __eq__(self, other)
!=         __ne__(self, other)


# Compound Assignment operators
=          __isub__(self, other)
+=         __iadd__(self, other)
*=         __imul__(self, other)
/=         __idiv__(self, other)
//=        __ifloordiv__(self, other)
%=         __imod__(self, other)
**=        __ipow__(self, other)
```

- Unlike many other languages like C++, Java, etc., Python does not support function overloading. It means function names in a program, or method names within a class must be unique.

Everything is an Object

```
import math
class Message :
    def display(self, msg):
        print(msg)


def fun( ) :
    print('Everything is an object')
```

```
i = 45
a = 3.14
c = 3 + 2j
city = 'Nagpur'
lst = [10, 20, 30]
tup = (10, 20, 30, 40)
s = {'a', 'e', 'i', 'o', 'u'}
d = { 'Ajay' : 30, 'Vijay' : 35, 'Sujay' : 36}

print(type(i), id(i))
print(type(a), id(a))
print(type(c), id(c))
print(type(city), id(city))
print(type(lst), id(lst))
print(type(tup), id(tup))
print(type(s), id(s))
print(type(d), id(d))
print(type(fun), id(fun))
print(type(Message), id(Message))
print(type(math), id(math))
```

On execution of this program we get the following output:

```
<class 'int'> 495245808
<class 'float'> 25154336
<class 'complex'> 25083752
<class 'str'> 25343392
<class 'list'> 25360544
<class 'tuple'> 25317808
<class 'set'> 20645208
<class 'dict'> 4969744
<class 'function'> 3224536
<class 'type'> 25347040
<class 'module'> 25352448
```

- In python every entity is an object. This includes int, float, bool, complex, string, list, tuple, set, dictionary, function, class, method and module.

- The **type( )** function returns type of the object, whereas **id( )** function returns location of the object in memory.

- Some objects are mutable, some are not. Also, all objects have some attributes and methods.

- Same object can have multiple names. We can change the object using one name, and access using other.

  ```
  i = 20
  j = i   # another name for same int object referred to by i
  k = i   # yet another name for same object
  k = 30
  print (i, j)   # will print 30 30 as i, j, k all are pointing to same object
  ```

- **x** and **y** are different objects. So changing one doesn't change the other.

  ```
  x = 20
  y = 20
  ```

Imitating a Structure

```
class Bird :
    pass


b = Bird( )


# create attributes dynamically
b.name = 'Sparrow'
b.weight = 500
b.color = 'light brown'
b.animaltype = 'Vertebrate'

# modify attributes
b.weight = 450
b.color = 'brown'

# delete attributes
del b.animaltype
```

- In C if we wish to keep dissimilar but related data together we create a structure do so.

- In Python too, we can do this by creating a class that is merely a collection of attributes (and not methods).

- Moreover, unlike C++ and Java, Python permits us to add / delete / modify these attributes to a class/object dynamically.

- In our program we have added 4 attributes, modified two attributes and deleted one attribute, all on the fly, i.e. after creation of **Bird** object.

Data Conversion

- There are three different types of data conversion that may exist. These are:

    (a) Conversion between different built-in types
    (b) Conversion between built-in and user-defined types
    (c) Conversion between different user-defined types

- Conversions between different built-in types

```
i = 125
a = float(i)   # int to float conversion
b = 3.14
j = int(b)     # float to int conversion
```

- Conversion between built-in and user-defined types

    Following program illustrates how a user-defined **String** type can be converted to built-in type **int**. **__int__( )** has been overloaded to carry out conversion from **str** to **int**.

```
class String :
    def __init__(self, s = '') :
        self._str = s

    def display(self) :
        print(self._str)

    def __int__(self) :
        return int( self._str )

s1 = String(123) # conversion from int to String
s1.display( )
i = int(s1)   # conversion from string to int
print(i)
```

- Conversion between different user-defined types

Following program illustrates how a user-defined **DMY** type can be converted to another user-defined type **Date**. **__Date__( )** has been overloaded to carry out conversion from **DMY** to **Date**.

```
class Date :
    def __init__(self, s = '') :
        self._dt = s

    def display(self) :
        print(self._dt)

class DMY :
    def __init__(self, d = 0, m = 0, y = 0 ) :
        self._day = d ;
        self._mth = m ;
        self._yr = y ;

    def __Date__( ) :
        s = str(self._day) + '/' + str(self._mth) + '/' + str(self._yr)
        return Date(s)

    def display(self) :
        print(self._day, '/', self._mth, '/', self._yr)

d2 = DMY( 17, 11, 94 )
d1 = d2 ;
print('d1 = ', end = '')
d1.display( )
print('d2 = ', end = '')
d2.display( )
```

Documentation Strings

- It is a good idea to mention a documentation string (often called doscstring) below a function, module, class or method definition. It should be the first line below the **def** or the **class** statement.

- The docstring available in the attribute **__doc__**.

- One-line docstrings should be written within triple quotes.

- Multi-line docstrings should contain a summary line followed by a blank line, followed by a detailed comment.

- Multi-line docstrings are also written within triple quotes.

- Using **help( )** method we can print the functions/class/method documentation systematically.

Iterators

- We know that container objects like string, list, tuple, set, dictionary etc. can be iterated through over using a for loop as in

```
for ch in 'Good Afternoon'
    print(ch)
for num in [01, 20, 30, 40, 50]
    print(num)
```

Both these **for** loops call **__iter__( )** method of **str/list**. This method returns an iterator object. The iterator object has a method **__next__( )** which returns the next item in the **str/list** container.

When all items have been iterated, next call to **__next__( )** raises a **StopIteration** exception which tells the **for** loop to terminate. Exceptions have been discussed in Chapter 15.

- We too can call **__iter__( )** and **__next__( )** and get the same results.

```
lst = [10, 20, 30, 40]
i = lst.__iter__( )
print(i.__next__( ))
print(i.__next__( ))
print(i.__next__( ))
```

- Instead of calling **__iter__( )** and **__next__( )**, we can call the more convenient **iter( )** and **next( )**. They in turn do call **__iter__( )** and **__next__( )** respectively.

```
lst = [10, 20, 30, 40]
i = iter(lst)
print(next(i))
print(next(i))
print(next(i))
```

Note than once we have iterated a container, if we wish to iterate it again we have to obtain an iterator object afresh.

- An iterable is an object capable of returning its members one at a time. Programmatically, it is an object that has implemented **__iter__( )** in it.

- An iterator is an object that has implemented both **__iter__( )** and **__next__( )** in it.

- As a proof that an iterable contains **__iter__( )**, whereas an iterator contains both **__iter__( )** and **__next__( )**, we can check it using the **hasattr( )** global function.

```
s = 'Hello'
lst = ['Focussed', 'bursts', 'of', 'activity']
print(hasattr(s, '__iter__'))
print(hasattr(s, '__next__'))
print(hasattr(lst, '__iter__'))
print(hasattr(lst, '__next__'))
i = iter(s)
j = iter(lst)
print(hasattr(i, '__iter__'))
print(hasattr(i, '__next__'))
print(hasattr(j, '__iter__'))
print(hasattr(j, '__next__'))
```

On execution of this program we get the following output:

```
True
False
True
False
True
True
True
True
```

User-defined Iterators

- Suppose we wish our class to behave like an iterator. To do this we need to define **__iter__( )** and **__next__( )** in it.

- Our iterator class **AvgAdj** should maintain a list. When it is iterated upon it should return average of two adjacent numbers in the list.

```
class AvgAdj :
    def __init__(self, data) :
        self._data = data
        self._len = len(data)
        self._first = 0
        self._second = 1

    def __iter__(self) :
        return self

    def __next__(self) :
        if self._second == self._len :
            raise StopIteration

        self._avg = (self._data[self._first] + self._data[self._second]) / 2
        self._first += 1
        self._second += 1
        return self._avg

lst = [10, 20, 30, 40, 50, 60, 70]
coll = AvgAdj(lst)

for val in coll :
    print(val)
```

On execution of this program, we get the following output:

```
15.0
25.0
35.0
45.0
55.0
65.0
```

- **__iter__( )** is supposed to return an object which has implemented **__next__( )** in it. Since we have defined **__next__( )** in **AvgAdj** class, we have returned **self** from **__iter__( )**.

- Length of **lst** is 7, whereas elements in it are indexed from 0 to 6.

- When **self._second** becomes 7 it means that we have reached the end of list and further iteration is not possible. In this situation we have raised an exception **StopIteration**.

Generators

- Generators are very efficient functions that create iterators. They use **yield** statement instead of **return** whenever they wish to return data from the function.

- Specialty of a generator is that, it remembers the state of the function and the last statement it had executed when **yield** was executed.

- So each time **next( )** is called, it resumes where it had left off last time.

- Generators can be used in place of class-based iterator that we saw in the last section.

- They are very compact because the **__iter__( )**, **__next__( )** and **StopIteration** code is created automatically for them.

```
def AvgAdj(data) :
    for i in range(0, len(data) - 1) :
        yield (data[i] + data[i + 1]) / 2

lst = [10, 20, 30, 40, 50, 60, 70]
for i in AvgAdj(lst) :
    print(i)
```

On execution of this program, we get the following output:

```
15.0
25.0
35.0
45.0
55.0
65.0
```

When to use Iterable and Iterator/Generator

- Suppose from a list of 100 integers we are to return an entity which contains elements which are prime numbers. In this case we will return an 'iterable' which contains a list of prime numbers.

- Suppose we wish to add all prime numbers below three million. In this case, first creating a list of all prime numbers and then adding them will consume lot of memory. So we should write a an iterator class or a generator function which generates prime numbers on the fly and adds it to the running sum.

Generator Expressions

- Like list comprehensions, to make the code more compact as well as succinct, we can write compact generator expressions.

- A generator expression creates a generator on the fly without being required to sue the **yield** statement.

- Some sample generator expressions are given below.

  ```
  # generate 20 random numbers in the range 10 to 100
  print(max(random.randint(10, 100) for n in range(20)))
  ```

  ```
  # print sum of cubes of all numbers less than 20
  print(sum(n * n * n for n in range(20)))
  ```

- Note that unlike list comprehensions which are enclosed within [ ], generator expressions are written within ( ).

- Since a list comprehension returns a list, it consumes more memory than a generator expression. Generator expression takes less memory since it generates the next element on demand, rather than generating all elements upfront.

  ```
  import sys
  lst = [i * i for i in range(15)]
  gen = (i * i for i in range(15))
  print(lst)
  print(gen)
  print(sys.getsizeof(lst))
  print(sys.getsizeof(gen))
  ```

  On execution of this program, we get the following output:

  ```
  [0, 1, 4, 9, 16, 25, 36, 49, 64, 81, 100, 121, 144, 169, 196]
  <generator object <genexpr> at 0x003BD570>
  100
  48
  ```

- Though useful, generator expressions do not have the same power of a full-fledged generator function.

p</> Programs

Problem 13.1

Write a Python function **display( )** to display a message and a function **show(msg1, msg2)** to display **msg1** in lowercase and **msg2** in uppercase. Use a single line docstring for **display( )** and a mulit-line docstring for **show( )**. Display both the docstrings. Also, generate help on both the functions.

Program

```
def display( ) :
    """Display a message."""
    print('Hello')
    print(display.__doc__)

def show(msg1 = ' ', msg2 = ' ') :
    """Display 2 messages.

    Arguments:
    msg1 -- message to be displayed in lowercase (default ' ')
    msg2 -- message to be displayed in uppercase (default ' ')
    """
    print(msg1.lower( ))
    print(msg2.upper( ))
    print(show.__doc__)

display( )
show('Cindrella', 'Mozerella')
help(display)
help(show)
```

Output

```
Hello
Display a message.
cindrella
MOZERELLA
Display 2 messages.

    Arguments:
    msg1 -- message to be displayed in lowercase (default ' ')
```

msg2 -- message to be displayed in uppercase (default ' ')

Help on function display in module __main__:

display( )
    Display a message.

Help on function show in module __main__:

show(msg1=' ', msg2=' ')
    Display 2 messages.

    Arguments:
    msg1 -- message to be displayed in lowercase (default ' ')

Problem 13.2

Create a class **Weather** that has a list containing weather parameters. Define an overloaded in operator that checks whether an item is present in the list.

Program

```
class Weather :
    def __init__(self) :
        self._params = [ 'Temp', 'Rel Hum', 'Cloud Cover', 'Wind Vel']
    def __contains__(self, p) :
        return True if p in self._params else False

w = Weather( )
if 'Rel Hum' in w :
    print('Valid weather parameter')
else :
    print('Invalid weather parameter')
```

Output

Valid weather parameter

Tips

- To overload the **in** operator we need to define the function **__contains__( )**.

Problem 13.3

Write a program that proves that a list is an iterable and not an iterator.

Program

```
lst = [10, 20, 30, 40, 50]
print(dir(lst))
i = iter(lst)
print(dir(i))
```

Output

['__add__', '__class__', '__contains__', '__delattr__', '__delitem__', '__dir__', '__doc__', '__eq__', '__format__', '__ge__', '__getattribute__', '__getitem__', '__gt__', '__hash__', '__iadd__', '__imul__', '__init__', '__init_subclass__', '__iter__', '__le__', '__len__', '__lt__', '__mul__', '__ne__', '__new__', '__reduce__', '__reduce_ex__', '__repr__', '__reversed__', '__rmul__', '__setattr__', '__setitem__', '__sizeof__', 'index', 'insert', 'pop', 'remove', 'reverse', 'sort']

['__class__', '__delattr__', '__dir__', '__doc__', '__eq__', '__format__', '__ge__', '__getattribute__', '__gt__', '__hash__', '__init__', '__init_subclass__', '__iter__', '__le__', '__length_hint__', '__lt__', '__ne__', '__new__', '__next__', '__reduce__', '__reduce_ex__', '__repr__', '__setattr__', '__setstate__', '__sizeof__', '__str__', '__subclasshook__']

Tips

- **lst** is an iterable since **dir(lst)** shows **__iter__** but no **__next__**.

- **iter(lst)** returns an iterator object, which is collected in **i**.

- **dir(i)** shows **__iter__** as well as **__next__**. This shows that it is an iterator object.

Problem 13.4

Write a program that generates prime numbers below 3 million. Print sum of these prime numbers.

Program

```
def generate_primes( ) :
```

```
    num = 1
    while True :
        if isprime(num) :
            yield num
        num += 1

def isprime( n ) :
    if n > 1 :
        if n == 2 :
            return True
        if n % 2 == 0 :
            return False
        for i in range(2, n // 2) :
            if n % i == 0 :
                return False
        else :
            return True
    else :
        return False

total = 0
for next_prime in generate_primes( ) :
    if next_prime < 300000 :
        total += next_prime
    else:
        print(total)
        exit( )
```

Output

3709507114

Tips

- **exit( )** terminates the execution of the program.

Problem 13.5

Write a program that uses generator expressions to print sin, cos and tan tables for angles ranging from 0 to 90 in steps of 30 degrees.

Program

```
import math
pi = 3.14
sine_table = {ang : math.sin(ang * pi / 180) for ang in range(0, 120, 30)}
cos_table = {ang : math.cos(ang * pi / 180) for ang in range(0, 120, 30)}
tan_table = {ang : math.tan(ang * pi / 180) for ang in range(0, 120, 30)}
print(sine_table)
print(cos_table)
print(tan_table)
```

Output

{0: 0.0, 30: 0.4997701026431024, 60: 0.8657598394923444, 90: 0.9999996829318346}
{0: 1.0, 30: 0.866158094405463, 60: 0.5004596890082058, 90: 0.0007963267107332633}
{0: 0.0, 30: 0.5769964003928729, 60: 1.72992922008979, 90: 1255.7655915007897}

Tips

- **exit( )** terminates the execution of the program.

 **Exercise**

[A] State whether the following statements are True or False:

(a) To carry out conversion from an object to a basic type or vice versa it is necessary to provide the conversion functions.

(b) To carry out conversion from object of one user-defined type to another it is necessary to provide the conversion functions.

(c) A global function can call a class method as well as an instance method.

(d) In Python a function, class, method and module are treated as objects.

(e) A generator is a function that serves the same purpose as an iterator.

[B] Answer the following:

(a) Which functions should be defined to overload the + and - operators?

(b) Which functions should be defined to overload the / and // operators?

(c) What is the purpose of **id( )** function?

(d) How will you define a structure **Employee** containing the attributes Name, Age, Salary, Address, Hobbies dynamically?

(e) Is it necessary to mention the docstring for a function immediately below the **def** statement?

[C] Match the following:

Cannot use as identifier name	class name
basic_salary	class variable
CellPhone	keyword
count	local variable in a function
self	private variable
_fuel_used	strongly private identifier
__draw( )	method that Python calls
__iter__( )	meaningful only in instance func.

[D] Attempt the following:

(a) Write a program that uses a generator to create a set of unique words from a line input through the keyboard.

(b) Write a program that uses a generator to find out maximum marks obtained by a student and his name from tuples of multiple students.

(c) Write a program that uses a generator that generates characters from a string in reverse order.

(d) Write a program that converts date maintained by **DMY** object into a date in **Date** object. Define the conversion function in **Date** class.

14 Inheritance

- Reuse Mechanisms
- Which to use When?
- Containership
- Inheritance
- What is Accessible where?
- *isinstance( )* and *issubclass( )*
- The *object* class
- Features of Inheritance
- Types of Inheritance
- Diamond Problem
- Abstract Classes
- Runtime Polymorphism
- Programs

Reuse Mechanisms

- Instead of reinventing the same code that is already available, it makes sense in reusing existing code.

- Python permits two code reuse mechanism:
  (a) Containership
  (b) Inheritance

- In both mechanisms we can reuse existing classes and create new enhanced classes based on them.

- We can reuse existing classes even if their source code is not available.

Which to use When?

- Containership should be used when the two classes have a 'has a' relationship. For example, a College has Professors. So **College** class's object can contain one or more **Professor** class's object(s).

- Inheritance should be used when the two classes have a 'like a' relationship. For example, a Button is like a Window. So **Button** class can inherit features of an existing class called **Window**.

Containership

- Containership is also known as composition. A container can contain one or more contained objects apart from other data.

```
class Department :
    def set_department(self) :
        self._id = input('Enter department id: ')
        self._name = input('Enter department name: ')

    def display_department(self) :
        print('Department ID is: ', self._id)
        print('Department Name is: ', self._name)

class Employee :
    def set_employee(self) :
        self._eid = input('Enter employee id: ')
```

```
        self._ename = input('Enter employee name: ')
        self._dobj = Department( )
        self._dobj.set_department( )

    def display_employee(self) :
        print('Employee ID : ', self._eid)
        print('Employee Name : ', self._ename)
        self._dobj.display_department( )

obj = Employee( )
obj.set_employee( )
obj.display_employee( )
```

Given below is the sample interaction with this program:

```
Enter employee id: 101
Enter employee name: Ramesh
Enter department id: ME
Enter department name: Mechanical Engineering
Employee ID : 101
Employee Name : Ramesh
Department ID is: ME
Department Name is: Mechanical Engineering
```

- In this program a **Department** object is contained in an **Employee** object.

Inheritance

- In Inheritance a new class called **derived** class can be created to inherit features of an existing class called **base** class.

- Base class is also called super class or parent class.

- Derived class is also called sub class or child class.

```
# base class
class Index :
    def __init__(self) :
    self._count = 0

    def display(self) :
        print('count = ' + str(self._count))
```

```
    def incr(self) :
        self._count += 1

# derived class
class NewIndex(Index) :
    def __init__(self) :
        super( ).__init__( )

    def decr(self) :
        self._count -= 1

i = NewIndex( )
i.incr( )
i.incr( )
i.incr( )
i.display( )
i.decr( )
i.display( )
i.decr( )
i.display( )
```

On execution of this program we get the following output:

```
count = 3
count = 2
count = 1
```

- Here, **Index** is the base class and **NewIndex** is the derived class.

- Construction of an object always proceeds from base towards derived.

- So when we create the derived class object, base class __init__( ) followed by derived class __init__( ) gets called. The syntax used for calling base class constructor is **super( ).__init__( )**.

- Derived class object contains all base class data. So **_count** is available in derived class.

- When **incr( )** is called using derived class object, first it is searched in derived class. Since it is not found here, the search is continued in the base class.

What is Accessible where?

- Derived class members can access base class members, vice versa is not true.

- In C++ three are private, protected and public keywords to control the access of base class members from derived class or from outside the class hierarchy. Python doesn't have any such keywords.

- Effect of private, protected and public is achieved by following a convention while creating variable names. This convention is shown below:

var - treat this as public variable
_var - treat this as protected variable
__var - treat this as private variable

Public variables may be accessed from anywhere.
Protected variables should be accessed only in class hierarchy.
Private variables should be used only in the class in which they are defined.

- Not using **_var** outside the class hierarchy is only a convention. If you violate it won't get errors, but it would be a bad practice to follow.

- However, any attempt to use __var either in the class hierarchy or outside the class, it would result in an error.

```python
class Base :
    def __init__(self) :
        self.i = 10
        self._a = 3.14
        self.__s = 'Hello'

    def display(self) :
        print ( self.i, self._a, self.__s)

class Derived(Base) :
    def __init__(self) :
        super( ).__init__( )
        self.i = 100
        self._a = 31.44
        self.__s = 'Good Morning'
        self.j = 20
```

```
            self._b = 6.28
            self.__ss = 'Hi'

    def display(self) :
        super( ).display( )
        print ( self.i, self._a, self.__s)
        print ( self.j, self._b, self.__ss)

dobj = Derived( )
dobj.display( )
print(dobj.i)
print(dobj._a)
print(dobj.__s)   # causes error

print(dobj.i)
print(dobj._a)
print(dobj.__s)   # causes error
```

On executing this program, we get the following output:

```
100
31.44
Hello
100
31.44
Good Morning
20
6.28
Hi
100
31.44
100
31.44
```

- In reality all __var type of variables get name mangled. i.e. in **Base** class __s becomes _base__s. Likewise, in **Derived** class __s becomes _Derived__s and __ss becomes _Derived__ss.

- When in **Derived** class's **Display( )** method we attempt to use __s, it is not the data member of **Base** class, but a new data member of **Derived** class that is being used.

isinstance( ) and *issubclass( )*

- **isinstance( )** and **issubclass( )** are global functions.

- **isinstance(o, c)** is used to check whether an object **o** is an instance of a class **c**.

- **issubclass(d, b)** is used to check whether class **d** has been derived from class **b**.

The *object* class

- All classes in Python are derived from a ready-made base class called **object**. So methods of this class are available in all classes.

- You can get a list of these methods using

```
print(dir(object))
print(dir(Index))
print(dir(NewIndex))
```

Features of Inheritance

- Inheritance facilitates three things:

    (a) Inheritance of existing feature: To implement this just establish inheritance relationship.

    (b) Suppressing an existing feature: Hide base class implementation by defining same method in derived class.

    (c) Extending an existing feature: call base class method from derived class by using one of the following two forms:

    ```
    super( ).base_class_method( )
    Baseclassname.base_class_method(self ) ;
    ```

Types of Inheritance

- There are 3 types of inheritance :

    (a) Simple Inheritance - Ex. class **NewIndex** derived from class **Index**

    (b) Multi-level Inheritance - Ex. class **HOD** is derived from class **Professor** which is derived from class **Person**.

    (c) Multiple Inheritance - Ex. class **HardwareSales** derived from two base classes—**Product** and **Sales**.

- In multiple inheritance, a class is derived from 2 or more than 2 base classes.

```python
class Product :
    def __init__(self) :
        self.title = input ('Enter title: ')
        self.price = input ('Enter price: ')

    def display_data(self) :
        print(self.title, self.price)

class Sales :
    def __init__(self) :
        self.sales_figures = [int(x) for x in input('Enter sales fig: ').split( )]

    def display_data(self) :
        print(self.sales_figures)

class HardwareItem(Product, Sales) :
    def __init__(self) :
        Product.__init__(self)
        Sales.__init__(self)
        self.category = input ('Enter category: ')
        self.oem = input ('Enter oem: ')

    def display_data(self) :
        Product.display_data(self)
        Sales.display_data(self)
        print(self.category, self.oem)

hw1 = HardwareItem( )
hw1.display_data( )
hw2 = HardwareItem( )
hw2.display_data( )
```

Given below is the sample interaction with this program:

```
Enter title: Bolt
Enter price: 12
Enter sales fig: 120 300 433
Enter category: C
Enter oem: Axis Mfg
```

Bolt 12
[120, 300, 433]
C Axis Mfg
Enter title: Nut
Enter price: 8
Enter sales fig: 1000 2000 1800
Enter category: C
Enter oem: Simplex Pvt Ltd
Nut 8
[1000, 2000, 1800]
C Simplex Pvt Ltd

- Note the syntax for calling **__init__( )** of base classes in the constructor of derived class:

  Product.__init__(self)
  Sales.__init__(self)

- We cannot use here the syntax **super.__init__( )**.

- Also not how the input for sales figures has been received using list comprehension.

Diamond Problem

- Suppose two classes Derived1 and Derived2 are derived from a base class called Base using simple inheritance. Also, a new class Der is derived from Derived1 and Derived2 using multiple inheritance. This is known as diamond relationship.

- If we now construct an object of **Der** it will have one copy of members from the path **Base -> Derived1** and another copy from the path **Base --> Derived2**. This will result in ambiguity.

- To eliminate the ambiguity, Python linearizes the search order in such a way that the left to right order while creating **Der** is honored. In our case it is **Derived1, Derived2**. So we would get a copy of members from the path **Base --> Derived1**.

```
class Base :
    def display(self) :
        print('In Base')

class Derived1(Base) :
    def display(self) :
```

```
        print('In Derived1')

class Derived2(Base) :
    def display(self) :
        print('In Derived2')

class Der(Derived1, Derived2) :
    def display(self) :
        super( ).display( )
        Derived1.display(self)
        Derived2.display(self)
        print(Der.__mro__)

d1 = Der( )
d1.display( )
```

On executing the program we get the following output:

```
In Derived2
In Derived1
In Derived2
(<class '__main__.Der'>, <class '__main__.Derived1'>, <class
'__main__.Derived2'>, <class '__main__.Base'>, <class 'object'>)
```

- **__mro__** gives the method resolution order.

Abstract Classes

- Suppose we have a **Shape** class and from it we have derived **Circle** and **Rectangle** classes. Each contains a method called **draw( )**. However, drawing a shape doesn't make too much sense, hence we do not want **draw( )** of **Shape** to ever get called. This can happen only if we can prevent creation of object of **Shape** class. This can be done as shown in the following program:

```
from abc import ABC, abstractmethod
class Shape(ABC) :
    @abstractmethod
    def draw(self) :
        pass

class Rectangle(Shape) :
    def draw(self) :
```

```
        print('In Rectangle.draw')

class Circle(Shape) :
    def draw(self) :
        print('In Circle.draw')

s = Shape( )    # will result in error, as Shape is abstract class
c = Circle( )
c.draw( )
```

- A class from which an object cannot be created is called an abstract class.

- **abc** stands for abstract base classes. To create an abstract class we need to derive it from class **ABC** present in **abc** module.

- Secondly, we need to mark **draw( )** as abstract method using the decorator **@abstractmethod**.

- If an abstract class contains only methods marked by the decorator **@abstractmethod**, it is often called an interface.

- Decorators are discussed in Chapter 17.

Runtime Polymorphism

- Polymorphism means one thing existing in several different forms. Runtime polymorphism involves deciding at runtime which function from base class or derived class should get called. This features is widely used in C++

- Parallel to Runtime Polymorphism, Java has a Dynamic Dispatch mechanism which works similarly.

- Since Python is dynamically typed language, where type of any variable is determined at runtime based on its usage, the discussion of Runtime Polymorphism or Dynamic Dispatch mechanism is not relevant for it.

Problem 14.1

Define a class **Shape**. Inherit two classes **Circle** and **Rectangle**. Check programmatically the inheritance relationship between the classes.

Create **Shape** and **Circle** objects. Report of which classes are these objects instances of.

Program

```
class Shape :
    pass
class Rectangle(Shape) :
    pass
class Circle(Shape) :
    pass

s = Shape( )
c = Circle( )
print(isinstance(s, Shape))
print(isinstance(s, Rectangle))
print(isinstance(s, Circle))
print(issubclass(Rectangle, Shape))
print(issubclass(Circle, Shape))
```

Output

```
True
False
False
True
True
```

Problem 14.2

Write a program that uses simple inheritance between classes **Base** and **Derived**. If there is a method in **Base** class, how do you prevent it from being overridden in the **Derived** class?

Program

```
class Base :
    def __method(self):
        print('In Base.__method')

    def func(self):
        self.__method( )
```

```
class Derived(Base):
    def __method(self):
        print('In Derived.__method')

b = Base( )
b.func( )
d = Derived( )
d.func( )
```

Output

In Base.__method
In Base.__method

Tips

- To prevent method from being overridden, prepend it with ___.

- When **func( )** is called using **b**, **self** contains address of **Base** class object. When it is called using **d**, **self** contains address of **Derived** class object.

- In **Base** class **__method( )** gets mangled to **_Base__method( )** and in **Derived** class it becomes **_Derived__method( )**.

- When **func( ) calls __method( )** from **Base** class, it is the **_Base__method( )** that gets called. In effect, **__method( )** cannot be overridden. This is true, even when **self** contains address of the **Derived** class object.

Problem 14.3

Write a program that defines a class called **Progression** and inherits three classes from it **AP**, **GP** and **FP**, standing for Arithmetic Progression, Geometric Progression and Fibonacci Progression respectively. **Progression** class should act as a user-defined iterator. By default, it should generate integers stating with 0 and advancing in steps of 1. **AP**, **GP** and **FP** should make use of the iteration facility of **Progression** class. They should appropriately adjust themselves to generate numbers in arithmetic progression, geometric progression or Fibonacci progression.

Program

```python
class Progression :
    def __init__ (self, start = 0) :
        self.cur = start

    def __iter__ (self):
        return self

    def advance(self):
        self.cur += 1

    def __next__ (self) :
        if self.cur is None :
            raise StopIteration
        else :
            data = self.cur
            self.advance( )
            return data

    def display(self, n) :
        print( ' '.join(str(next(self)) for i in range(n)))

class AP(Progression) :
    def __init__ (self, start = 0, step = 1) :
        super( ).__init__ (start)
        self.step = step

    def advance(self) :
        self.cur += self.step

class GP(Progression) :
    def __init__ (self, start = 1, step = 2 ) :
        super( ).__init__(start)
        self.step = step

    def advance(self) :
        self.cur *= self.step

class FP(Progression) :
    def __init__ (self, first = 0, second = 1) :
        super( ).__init__(first)
```

```
            self.prev = second - first

    def advance(self) :
        self.prev, self.cur = self.cur, self.prev + self.cur

print('Default progression:')
p = Progression( )
p.display(10)
print('AP with step 5:')
a = AP(5)
a.display(10)
print('AP with start 2 and step 4:')
a = AP(2, 4)
a.display(10)
print('GP with default multiple:')
g = GP( )
g.display(10)
print('GP with start 1 and multiple 3:')
g = GP(1, 3)
g.display(10)
print('FP with default start values:')
f = FP( )
f.display(10)
print('FP with start values 4 and 6:')
f = FP(4, 6)
f.display(10)
```

Output

```
Default progression:
0 1 2 3 4 5 6 7 8 9
AP with step 5:
5 6 7 8 9 10 11 12 13 14
AP with start 2 and step 4:
2 6 10 14 18 22 26 30 34 38
GP with default multiple:
1 2 4 8 16 32 64 128 256 512
GP with start 1 and multiple 3:
1 3 9 27 81 243 729 2187 6561 19683
FP with default start values:
0 1 1 2 3 5 8 13 21 34
FP with start values 4 and 6:
```

4 6 10 16 26 42 68 110 178 288

Tips

- Since **Progression** is an iterator it has to implement **__iter__( )** and **__next__( )** methods.

- **__next__( )** calls **advance( )** method to suitably adjust the value of **self.cur** (and **self.prev** in case of **FP**).

- Each derived class has an **advance( )** method. Depending on which object's address is present in **self**, that object's **advance( )** method gets called.

- The generation of next data value happens one value at a time, when **display( )** method's **for** loop goes into action.

- There are two ways to create an object and call **display( )**. These are:
  a = AP(5)
  a.display(10)

  or

  AP(5).display(10)

Problem 14.4

Write a program that defines an abstract class called **Printer** containing an abstract method **print( )**. Derive from it two classes—**LaserPrinter** and **Inkjetprinter**. Create objects of derived classes and call the **print( )** method using these objects, passing to it the name of the file to be printed. In the **print( )** method simply print the filename and the class name to which **print( )** belongs.

Program

```
from abc import ABC, abstractmethod
class Printer(ABC) :
    def __init__(self, n) :
        self.name = n

    @abstractmethod
    def print(self, docName) :
        pass
```

```
class LaserPrinter(Printer) :
    def __init__(self, n) :
        super( ).__init__(n)

    def print(self, docName) :
        print('>> LaserPrinter.print')
        print('Trying to print :', docName)

class InkjetPrinter(Printer) :
    def __init__(self, n) :
        super( ).__init__(n)

    def print(self, docName) :
        print('>> InkjetPrinter.print')
        print('Trying to print :', docName)

p = LaserPrinter('LaserJet 1100')
p.print('hello1.pdf')
p = InkjetPrinter('IBM 2140')
p.print('hello2.doc')
```

Output

```
>> LaserPrinter.print
Trying to print :
hello1.pdf
>> InkjetPrinter.print
Trying to print :
hello2.doc
```

Problem 14.5

Define an abstract class called **Character** containing an abstract method **patriotism( )**. Define a class **Actor** containing a method **style( )**. Define a class **Person** derived from **Character** and **Actor**. Implement the method **patriotism( )** in it, and override the method **style( )** in it. Also define a new method **do_acting( )** in it. Create an object of **Person** class and call the three methods in it.

Program

```
from abc import ABC, abstractmethod
```

```
class Character(ABC) :
    @abstractmethod
    def patriotism(self) :
        pass

class Actor :
    def style(self) :
        print('>> Actor.Style: ')

class Person(Actor, Character) :
    def do_acting(self) :
        print('>> Person.doActing')

    def style(self) :
        print('>> Person.style')

    def patriotism(self) :
        print('>> Person.patriotism')

p = Person( )
p.patriotism( )
p.style( )
p.do_acting( )
```

Output

```
>> Person.patriotism
>> Person.style
>> Person.doActing
```

 Exercise

[A] State whether the following statements are True or False:

(a) Inheritance is the ability for a class to inherit properties and behavior from a parent class by extending it.

(b) Containership is the ability of a class to contain objects of different classes as member data.

(c) We can derive a class from a base class even if the base class's source code is not available.

(d) Multiple inheritance is different from multiple levels of inheritance.

(e) An object of a derived class cannot access members of base class is the member names begin with ___.

(f) Creating a derived class from a base class requires fundamental changes to the base class.

(g) If a base class contains a member function **func( )**, and a derived class does not contain a function with this name, an object of the derived class cannot access **func( )**.

(h) If no constructors are specified for a derived class, objects of the derived class will use the constructors in the base class.

(i) If a base class and a derived class each include a member function with the same name, the member function of the derived class will be called by an object of the derived class.

(j) A class **D** can be derived from a class **C**, which is derived from a class **B**, which is derived from a class **A**.

(k) It is illegal to make objects of one class members of another class.

[B] Answer the following:

(a) Which module should be imported to create abstract class?

(b) For a class to be abstract from which class should we inherit it?

(c) Implement a **String** class containing the following functions:

– Overloaded += operator function to perform string concatenation.
– Method **toLower( )** to convert upper case letters to lower case.
– Method **toUpper( )** to convert lower case letters to upper case.

(d) Suppose there is a base class **B** and a derived class **D** derived from B. B has two **public** member functions **b1( )** and **b2( )**, whereas **D** has two member functions **d1( )** and **d2( )**. Write these classes for the following different situations:

– **b1( )** should be accessible from main module, **b2( )** should not be.
– Neither **b1( )**, nor **b2( )** should be accessible from main module.

    — Both **b1( )** and **b2( )** should be accessible from main module.

(e) If a class **D** is derived from two base classes **B1** and **B2**, then write these classes each containing a constructor. Ensure that while building an object of type **D**, constructor of **B2** should get called. Also provide a destructor in each class. In what order would these destructors get called?

(f) Create an abstract class called **Vehicle** containing methods **speed( )**, **maintenance( )** and **value( )** in it. Derive classes **FourWheeler**, **TwoWheeler** and **Airborne** from **Vehicle** class. Check whether you are able to prevent creation of objects of **Vehicle** class. Call the methods using objects of other classes.

(g) Assume a class **D** that is derived from class **B**. Which of the following can an object of class **D** access?
    — members of **D**
    — members of **B**

[C] Match the following:

__mro__( )	'has a' relationship
Inheritance	Object creation not allowed
__var	Super class
abstract class	Root class
Parent class	'is a' relationship
object	Name mangling
Child class	Decides resolution order
Containership	Sub class

15 Exception Handling

183

What may go Wrong?

- While creating and executing a Python program things may go wrong at two different stages—during compilation and during execution.

- Errors that occur during compilation are called Syntax errors. Errors that occur during execution are called Exceptions.

Syntax Errors

- If things go wrong during compilation:

  Means - Something in the program is not as per language grammar
  Reported by - Interpreter/Compiler
  Action to be taken - Rectify program

- Examples of syntax errors:

  ```
  print 'Hello'   # ( ) is missing
  d = 'Nagpur'
  a = b + float(d)   # d is a string, so it cannot be converted to float
  a = Math.pow(3)  # pow( ) needs two arguments
  ```

- Other common syntax error are:
  - Leaving out a symbol, such as a colon, comma or brackets
  - Misspelling a keyword
  - Incorrect indentation
  - Empty if, else, while, for, function, class, method
  - Missing :
  - Incorrect number of positional arguments

- Suppose we try to compile the following piece of code:

  ```
  basic_salary = input('Enter basic salary')
  if basic_salary < 5000
      print('Does not qualify for Diwali bonus')
  ```

  We get the following syntax error:

  ```
  File 'c:\Users\Kanetkar\Desktop\Phone\src\phone.py', line 2
      if basic_salary < 5000
                            ^
  ```

SyntaxError: invalid syntax

- ^ indicates the position in the line where an error was detected. it occurred because : is missing after the condition.

- Filename and line number are also displayed to help you locate the erroneous statement easily.

Exceptions

- If things go wrong during execution (runtime):

  Means - Something unforeseen has happened
  Reported by - Python Runtime
  Action to be taken - Tackle it on the fly

- Examples of Runtime errors:

  Memory Related - Stack / Heap overflow, Exceeding array bounds
  Arithmetic Related - Divide by zero, Arithmetic overflow/underflow
  Others - Attempt to use an unassigned reference, File not found

- Even if the program is grammatically correct, things may go wrong during execution causing exceptions.

  ```
  a = int(input('Enter an integer: '))
  b = int(input('Enter an integer: '))
  c = a / b
  ```

  If during execution of this script we give value of **b** as 0, then following message gets displayed:

  ```
  Exception has occurred: ZeroDivisionError
  division by zero
  File 'C:\Users\Kanetkar\Desktop\Phone\src\trial.py', line 3, in
  <module> c = a / b
  # blah blah blah ..rest of the stack trace
  ```

- Another example of exception:

  ```
  a, b = 10, 20
  c = a / b * d
  ```

  ```
  File 'c:\Users\Kanetkar\Desktop\Phone\src\phone.py', line 2, in
  <module>   c = a / b * d
  NameError: name 'd' is not defined
  # blah blah blah ..rest of the stack trace
  ```

- The stack trace prints the names of the files, line numbers starting from the first file that got executed, up to the point of exception.

- The stack trace is useful for the programmer to figure out where things went wrong. However a user is likely to get spooked looking at it, thinking something is very wrong. So we should try and tackle the exceptions ourselves and provide a graceful exit from the program, instead of printing the stack trace.

How to deal with Exceptions?

- **try** and **except** blocks are used to deal with an exception.

- Statement(s) which you suspect may go wrong at runtime should be enclosed within a **try** block.

- If while executing statement(s) in **try** block, an exceptional condition occurs it can be tackled in 2 Ways:

  (a) Pack exception information in an object and raise an exception.
  (b) Let Python Runtime pack exception information in an object and raise an exception. (in the above examples Python runtime raised exceptions **ZeroDivisionError** and **NameError**.)

  Raising an exception is same as throwing an exception in C++/Java.

- Two things that can be done when an exception is raised:

  (a) Catch the raised exception object in **except** block.
  (b) Raise the exception further.

- If we catch the exception object, we can either perform a graceful exit or rectify the exceptional situation and continue.

- If we raise the exception object further - Default exception handler catches the object, prints Stack Trace and terminates.

- Two ways to create exception objects:

  (a) From ready-made exception classes (like **ZeroDivisionError**)
  (b) From user-defined exception classes

- Advantage of tackling exceptions in OO manner:

  - More information can be packed into Exception objects.
  - Propagation of exception objects from the point where they are raised to the point where they are tackled is managed by Python Runtime.

- How Python facilitates exception handling:

- By providing keywords **try, except, else, finally, raise**.
- By providing readymade exception classes.

How to use *try - except*?

- **try** block - Enclose in it the code that you anticipate will cause an exception.

- **except** block - Catch the raised exception in it. It must immediately follow the **try** block.

```
try :
    a = int(input('Enter an integer: '))
    b = int(input('Enter an integer: '))
    c = a / b
    print('c =', c)
except ZeroDivisionError :
    print('Denominator is 0')
```

Given below is the sample interaction with the program:

```
Enter an integer: 10
Enter an integer: 0
Denominator is 0
```

- If no exception occurs while executing the **try** block, control goes to first line beyond the **except** block.

- If an exception occurs during execution of statements in **try** block, an exception is raised and rest of the **try** block is skipped. Control now goes to the **except** block. Here, if the type of exception raised matches the exception named after **except** keyword, that **except** block is executed.

- If an exception occurs which does not match the exception named in **except** block, then the default exception handler catches the exception, prints stack trace and terminates execution.

- When exception is raised and **except** block is executed, control goes to the next line after **except** block, unless there is a **return** or **raise** in **except** block.

Nuances of *try* and *except*

- **try** block:
    - Can be nested inside another **try** block.

- If an exception occurs and if a matching except handler is not found in the **except** block, then the outer try's **except** handlers are inspected for a match.

- **except** block:
    - Multiple **except** blocks for one **try** block are OK.
    - At a time only one **except** block goes to work.
    - If same action is to be taken in case of multiple exceptions, then the except clause can mention these exceptions in a tuple

    ```
    try :
        # some statements
    except (NameError, TypeError, ZeroDivisionError) :
        # some other statements
    ```

    - Order of **except** blocks is important - Derived first, Base last.
    - An empty **except** is like a catchall—catches all exceptions.
    - An exception may be re-raised from any except block.

- Given below is a program that puts some of the try, except nuances to a practical stint:

```
try :
    a = int(input('Enter an integer: '))
    b = int(input('Enter an integer: '))
    c = a / b
    print('c =', c)
except ZeroDivisionError as zde :
    print('Denominator is 0')
    print(zde.args)
    print(zde)
except ValueError :
    print('Unable to convert string to int')
except :
    print('Some unknown error')
```

Given below is the sample interaction with the program:

```
Enter an integer: 10
Enter an integer: 20
c = 0.5
```

```
Enter an integer: 10
Enter an integer: 0
Denominator is 0
```

('division by zero',)
division by zero

Enter an integer: 10
Enter an integer: abc
Unable to convert string to int

- If an exception occurs, the type of exception raised is matched with the exceptions named after **except** keyword. When a match occurs, that **except** block is executed, and then execution continues after the last **except** block.

- If we wish to do something more before doing a graceful exit, we can use the keyword **as** to receive the exception object. We can then access its argument either using its **args** variable, or by simply using the exception object.

- **args** actually refers to arguments that were used while creating the exception object.

User-defined Exceptions

- Since all exceptional conditions cannot be anticipated, for every exceptional condition there cannot be a class in Python library.

- In such cases we can define our own exception class as shown in the following program:

```
class InsufficientBalanceError(Exception) :
    def __init__(self, accno, cb) :
    self.accno = accno
        self.curbal = cb

    def get_details(self) :
        return { 'Acc no' : self.accno, 'Current Balance' : self.curbal}

class Customers :
    def __init__(self) :
        self.dct = { }

    def append(self, accno, n, bal) :
        self.dct[accno] = { 'Name' : n, 'Balance' : bal }

    def deposit(self, accno, amt) :
```

```
        d = self.dct[accno]
        d['Balance'] = d['Balance'] + amt
        self.dct[accno] = d

    def display(self) :
        for k, v in self.dct.items( ) :
            print(k, v)
        print( )

    def withdraw(self, accno, amt) :
        d = self.dct[accno]
        curbal = d['Balance']
        if curbal - amt < 5000 :
            raise InsufficientBalanceError(accno, curbal)
        else :
            d['Balance'] = d['Balance'] - amt
            self.dct[accno] = d

c = Customers( )
c.append(123, 'Sanjay', 9000)
c.append(101, 'Sameer', 8000)
c.append(423, 'Ajay', 7000)
c.append(133, 'Sanket', 6000)
c.display( )

c.deposit(123, 1000)
c.deposit(423, 2000)
c.display( )

try :
    c.withdraw(423, 3000)
    print('Amount withdrawn successfully')
    c.display( )
    c.withdraw(101, 5000)
    print('Amount withdrawn successfully')
    c.display( )
except InsufficientBalanceError as ibe :
    print('Withdrawal denied')
    print('Insufficient balance')
    print(ibe.get_details( ))
```

On execution of this program we get the following output:

123 {'Name': 'Sanjay', 'Balance': 9000}
101 {'Name': 'Sameer', 'Balance': 8000}
423 {'Name': 'Ajay', 'Balance': 7000}
133 {'Name': 'Sanket', 'Balance': 6000}

123 {'Name': 'Sanjay', 'Balance': 10000}
101 {'Name': 'Sameer', 'Balance': 8000}
423 {'Name': 'Ajay', 'Balance': 9000}
133 {'Name': 'Sanket', 'Balance': 6000}

Amount withdrawn successfully
123 {'Name': 'Sanjay', 'Balance': 10000}
101 {'Name': 'Sameer', 'Balance': 8000}
423 {'Name': 'Ajay', 'Balance': 6000}
133 {'Name': 'Sanket', 'Balance': 6000}

Withdrawal denied
Insufficient balance
{'Acc no': 101, 'Current Balance': 8000}

- Each customer in a Bank has data like account number, name and balance amount. This data is maintained in nested directories.

- If during withdrawal of money from a particular account if the balance goes below Rs. 5000, then a user-defined exception called **InsufficientBalanceError** is raised.

- In the matching **except** block, details of the withdrawal transaction that resulted into an exception are fetched by calling **get_details( )** method present in **InsufficientBalanceError** class and displayed.

- **get_details( )** returns the formatted data. If we wish to get raw data, then we can use **ibe.args** variable, or simply **ibe**.
  print(ibe.args)
  print(ibe)

else Block

- The **try** .. **except** statement may also have an optional **else** block.

- If it is present, it must occur after all the **except** blocks.

- Control goes to **else** block if no exception occurs during execution of the **try** block.

```
try :
    lst = [10, 20, 30, 40, 50]
    for num in lst :
        i = int(num)
        j = i * i
        print(i, j)
except NameError:
    print(NameError.args)
else:
    print('Total numbers processed', len(lst))
    del(lst)
```

We get the following output on executing this program:

```
10 100
20 400
30 900
40 1600
50 2500
Total numbers processed 5
```

- Control goes to **else** block since no exception occurred while obtaining squares.

- If we replace one of the elements to say 'abc', then a **NameError** will occur which will be caught by **except** block. In this case **else** block doesn't go to work.

finally **Block**

- **finally** block is optional.

- Code in **finally** always runs, no matter what! Even if a **return** or **break** occurs first.

- **finally** block is placed after **except** blocks (if they exist).

- **try** block must have **except** block and/or **finally** block.

- **finally** block is commonly used for releasing external resources like files, network connections or database connections, irrespective of whether the use of the resource was successful or not.

Exception Handling Tips

- Don't catch and ignore an exception.

- Don't catch everything using a catchall except, distinguish between types of exceptions.

- Make it optimally elaborate - Not too much, not too little.

Problem 15.1

Write a program that infinitely receives positive integer as input and prints its square. If a negative number is entered then raise an exception, display a relevant error message and make a graceful exit.

Program

```
try:
    while True :
        num = int(input('Enter a positive number: '))
        if num >= 0 :
            print(num * num)
        else :
            raise ValueError('Negative number')
except ValueError as ve :
    print(ve.args)
```

Output

```
Enter a positive number: 12
144
Enter a positive number: 34
1156
Enter a positive number: 45
2025
Enter a positive number: -9
('Negative number',)
```

Problem 15.2

Write a program that implements a stack data structure of specified size. If the stack becomes full and we still try to push an element to it, then an **IndexError** exception should be raised. Similarly, if the stack is empty and we try to pop an element from it then an **IndexError** exception should be raised.

Program

```
class Stack :
    def __init__(self, sz) :
        self.size = sz
        self.arr = [ ]
        self.top = -1

    def push(self, n) :
        if self.top + 1 == self.size :
            raise IndexError('Stack is full')
        else :
            self.top += 1
            self.arr = self.arr + [n]

    def pop(self) :
        if self.top == -1 :
            raise IndexError('Stack is empty')
        else :
            n = self.arr[self.top]
            self.top -= 1
            return n

    def printall(self) :
        print(self.arr)

s = Stack(5)
try :

    s.push(10)
    n = s.pop( )
    print(n)
    n = s.pop( )
    print(n)
    s.push(20)
    s.push(30)
    s.push(40)
    s.push(50)
    s.push(60)
```

```
        s.printall( )
        s.push(70)
except IndexError as ie :
    print(ie.args)
```

Output

```
10
('Stack is empty',)
```

Tips

- A new element is added to the stack by merging two lists.

- **IndexError** is a readymade exception class. Here we have used it to raise a stack full or stack empty exception.

Problem 15.3

Write a program that implements a queue data structure of specified size. If the queue becomes full and we still try to add an element to it, then a user-defined **QueueError** exception should be raised. Similarly, if the queue is empty and we try to delete an element from it then a **QueueError** exception should be raised.

Program

```
class QueueError(Exception) :
    def __init__(self, msg, front, rear ) :
        self.errmsg = msg + ' front = ' + str(front) + ' rear = ' + str(rear)

    def get_message(self) :
        return self.errmsg

class Queue :
    def __init__(self, sz) :
        self.size = sz
        self.arr = [ ]
        self.front = self.rear = -1

    def add_queue(self, item) :
        if self.rear == self.size - 1 :
            raise QueueError('Queue is full.', self.front, self.rear)
```

```
        else :
            self.rear += 1
            self.arr = self.arr + [item]

            if self.front == -1 :
                self.front = 0

    def delete_queue(self) :
        if self.front == -1 :
            raise QueueError('Queue is empty.', self.front, self.rear)
        else :
            data = self.arr[self.front]
            if ( self.front == self.rear ) :
                self.front = self.rear = -1
            else :
                self.front += 1

            return data

    def printall(self) :
        print(self.arr)

q = Queue(5)
try :
    q.add_queue(11)
    q.add_queue(12)
    q.add_queue(13)
    q.add_queue(14)
    q.add_queue(15) # oops, queue is full
    q.printall( )

    i = q.delete_queue( )
    print('Item deleted = ', i)
    i = q.delete_queue( )
    print('Item deleted = ', i)
    i = q.delete_queue( )
    print('Item deleted = ', i)
    i = q.delete_queue( )
    print('Item deleted = ', i)
    i = q.delete_queue( )
    print('Item deleted = ', i)
```

```
    i = q.delete_queue( ) # oops, queue is empty
    print('Item deleted = ', i)

except QueueError as qe :
    print(qe.get_message( ))
```

Output

```
[11, 12, 13, 14, 15]
Item deleted =  11
Item deleted =  12
Item deleted =  13
Item deleted =  14
Item deleted =  15
Queue is empty. front = -1 rear = -1
```

Problem 15.4

Write a program that receives an integer as input. If a string is entered instead of an integer, then report an error and give another chance to user to enter an integer. Continue this process till correct input is supplied.

Program

```
while True :
    try :
        num = int(input('Enter a number: '))
        break
    except ValueError :
        print('Incorrect Input')

print('You entered: ', num)
```

Output

```
Enter a number: aa
Incorrect Input
Enter a number: abc
Incorrect Input
Enter a number: a
Incorrect Input
Enter a number: 23
```

You entered: 23

 Exercise

[A] State whether the following statements are True or False:

(a) The exception handling mechanism is supposed to handle compile time errors.

(b) It is necessary to declare the exception class within the class in which an exception is going to be thrown.

(c) Every raised exception must be caught.

(d) For one **try** block there can be multiple **except** blocks.

(e) When an exception is raised an exception class's constructor gets called.

(f) **try** blocks cannot be nested.

(g) Proper destruction of an object is guaranteed by exception handling mechanism.

(h) All exceptions occur at runtime.

(i) Exceptions offer an object-oriented way of handling runtime errors.

(j) If an exception occurs, then the program terminates abruptly without getting any chance to recover from the exception.

(k) No matter whether an exception occurs or not, the statements in the **finally** clause (if present) will get executed.

(l) A program can contain multiple **finally** clauses.

(m) **finally** clause is used to perform cleanup operations like closing the network/database connections.

(n) While raising a user-defined exception multiple values can be set in the exception object.

(o) In one function/method, there can be only one **try** block.

(p) An exception must be caught in the same function/method in which it is raised.

(q) All values set up in the exception object are available in the **except** block.

(r) If our program does not catch an exception then the Python Runtime catches it.

(s) It is possible to create user-defined exceptions.

(t) All types of exceptions can be caught using the **Exception** class.

(u) For every **try** block there must be a corresponding **finally** block.

[B] Answer the following:

(a) If we do not catch the exception thrown at runtime then who will catch it?

(b) Explain in short most compelling reasons for using exception handling over conventional error handling approaches.

(c) Is it necessary that all classes that can be used to represent exceptions be derived from base class **Exception**?

(d) What is the use of a **finally** block in Python exception handling sequence?

(e) How does nested exception handling work in Python?

(f) Write a program that receives 10 integers and stores them and their cubes in a dictionary. If the number entered is less than 3, raise a user-defined exception **NumberTooSmall**, and if the number entered is more than 30, then raise a user-defined exception **NumberTooBig**. Whether an exception occurs or not, at the end print the contents of the dictionary.

(g) What's wrong with the following code snippet?

```
try :
    # some statements
```

```
except :
    # report error 1
except ZeroDivisionError :
    # report error 2
```

(h) Which of these keywords is not part of Python's exception handling—**try, catch, throw, raise, finally, else**?

(i) What will be the output of the following code?

```
def fun( ) :
    try :
        return 10
    finally :
        return 20

k = fun( )
print(k)
```

16

File Input/Output

- I/O System

- File I/O

- Read / Write Operations

- File Opening Modes

- *with* Keyword

- Moving within a File

- Serialization and Deserialization

- Serialization of User-defined Types

- File and Directory Operations

- Programs

- Exercise

201

I/O System

- Expectations from an I/O System:

    - I should be able to communicate with sources & destinations.
      Ex. Sources - Keyboard, File, Network
      Ex. Destinations - Screen, File, Network

    - I should be able to I/O varied entities.
      Ex. Numbers, Strings, Lists, Tuples, Sets, Dictionaries, etc.

    - I should be able to communicate in multiple ways.
      Ex. Sequential access, Random access

    - I should be able to deal with underlying file system.
      Ex. Create, modify, rename, delete files and directories

- Types of data used for I/O:

    Text - '485000' as a sequence of Unicode characters.
    Binary - 485000 as sequence of bytes of its binary equivalent.

- File Types:

    All program files are text files.
    All image, music, video, executable files are binary files.

File I/O

- Sequence of operations in File I/O:

    - Open a file
    - Read/Write data to it
    - Close the file

```
# write/read text data
msg1 = 'Pay taxes with a smile...\n'
msg2 = 'I tried, but they wanted money!\n'
msg3 = 'Don\'t feel bad...\n'
msg4 = 'It is alright to have no talent!\n'

f = open('messages', 'w')
f.write(msg1)
f.write(msg2)
f.write(msg3)
f.write(msg4)
```

```
f.close( )

f = open('messages', 'r')
data = f.read( )
print(data)
f.close( )
```

On executing this program, we get the following output:

Pay taxes with a smile...
I tried, but they wanted money!
Don't feel bad...
It is alright to have no talent!

- Opening a file brings its contents to a buffer in memory. While performing read/write operations, data is read from or written to buffer.

```
f = open(filename, 'r')  # opens file for reading
f = open(filename, 'w')  # opens file for writing
f.close( )  # closes the file by vacating the buffer
```

  Once file is closed read/write operation on it are not feasible.

- **f.write( )** writes a new string each time to the file.

- **data = f.read( )** reads all the lines into **data**.

Read / Write Operations

- There are two functions for writing data to a file:

```
msg = 'Bad officials are elected by good citizens who do not vote.\n'
msgs = ['Humpty\n', 'Dumpty\n', 'Sat\n', 'On\n', 'a\n', 'wall\n']
f.write(msg)
f.writelines(msgs)
```

- To write objects other than strings, we need to convert them to strings before writing:

```
tpl = ('Ajay', 23, 15000)
s = { 23, 45, 56, 78, 90 }
d = { 'Name' : 'Dilip', 'Age' : 25}
f.write(str(tpl))
f.write(str(s))
f.write(str(d))
```

- There are three functions for reading data from a file represented by file object **f**.

```
data = f.read( )       # reads entire file contents and returns as string
data = f.read(n)       # reads n characters, and returns as string
data = f.readline( )   # reads a line, and returns as string
```

If end of file is reached **f.read( )** returns an empty string.

- There are two ways to read a file line-by-line till end of file:

```
# first way
while True :
    data = f.readline( )
    if data == " " :
        break
print(data, end ='')

# second way
for data in f :
    print(data, end ='')
```

- To read all the lines in a file and form a **list** of lines:

```
data = f.readlines( )
data = list(f)
```

File Opening Modes

- There are multiple file-opening modes available:

  'r' - Opens file for reading in text mode.
  'w' - Opens file for writing in text mode.
  'a' - Opens file for appending in text mode.

  'rb' - Opens file for reading in text mode.
  'wb' - Opens file for writing in text mode.
  'ab' - Opens file for appending in text mode.

  'r+', 'rb+' - Opens file for reading and writing.
  'w+', 'wb+' - Opens file for reading and writing.
  'a+', 'ab+' - Opens file for appending and reading.

  If mode argument is not mentioned while opening a file, then 'r' is assumed.

- While opening a file for writing, if the file already exists, it is overwritten.

with Keyword

- It is a good idea to close a file once its usage is over, as it will free up system resources.

- If we don't close a file, when the file object is destroyed file will be closed for you by Python's garbage collector program.

- If we use **with** keyword while opening the file, the file gets closed as soon as its usage is over.

  with open('messages', 'r') as f :
      data = f.read( )

- **with** ensures that the file is closed even if an exception occurs while processing it.

Moving within a File

- When we are reading a file or writing a file, the next read or write operation is performed from the next character/byte as compared to the previous read/write operation.

- Thus if we read the first character from a file using **f.read(1)**, next call to **f.read(1)** will automatically be the second character in the file.

- At times we may wish to move to desired position in a file before reading/writing. This can be done using **f.seek( )** method.

- General form of **seek( )** is given below:

  f.seek(offset, reference)

  reference can take values 0, 1, 2 standing for beginning, of file, current position in file and end of file respectively.

- For file opened in text mode, reference values 0 and 2 alone can be used. Also, using 2, we can only move to end of file.

  f.seek(512, 0)   # moves to position 512 from beginning of file
  f.seek(0, 2)   # moves to end of file

- For file opened in binary mode, reference values 0, 1, 2 can be used.

  f.seek(12, 0)   # moves to position 12 from beginning of file
  f.seek(-15, 2)   # moves to position 15 from end of file
  f.seek(6, 1)   # moves 6 positions to right from current position
  f.seek(-10, 1)   # moves 10 positions to left from current position

Serialization and Deserialization

- Compared to strings, reading/writing numbers from/to a file is tedious. This is because **write( )** writes a string to a file and **read( )** returns a string read from a file. So we need to do conversions while reading/writing, as shown in the following program:

```
f = open('numberstxt', 'w+')
f.write(str(233)+'\n')
f.write(str(13.45))
f.seek(0)
a = int(f.readline( ))
b = float(f.readline( ))
print(a + a)
print(b + b)
```

- If we are read/write more complicated data in the form of tuple, dictionaries, etc. from/to file it will become more difficult. In such cases a module called **json** should be used.

- **json** module converts Python data into appropriate JSON types before writing data to a file. Likewise, it converts JSON types read from a file into Python data. The first process is called **serialization** and the second is called **deserialization**.

```
# serialize/deserialize a list
import json
f = open('sampledata', 'w+')
lst = [10, 20, 30, 40, 50, 60, 70, 80, 90]
json.dump(lst, f)
f.seek(0)
inlst = json.load(f)
print(inlst)
f.close( )
```

```
# serialize/deserialize a tuple
import json
f = open('sampledata', 'w+')
tpl = ('Ajay', 23, 2455.55)
json.dump(tpl, f)
f.seek(0)
intpl = json.load(f)
```

```
print(tuple(intpl))
f.close( )

# serialize/deserialize a dictionary
import json
f = open('sampledata', 'w+')
dct = { 'Anil' : 24, 'Ajay' : 23, 'Nisha' : 22}
json.dump(dct, f)
f.seek(0)
indct = json.load(f)
print(indct)
f.close( )
```

- Serialization of a Python type to JSON data is done using a function **dump( )**. It writes the serialized data to a file.

- Deserialization of a JSON type to a Python type is done using a function **load( )**. It reads the data from a file, does the conversion and returns the converted data.

- While deserializing a tuple, **load( )** returns a list and not a tuple. So we need to convert the list to a tuple using **touple( )** conversion function.

- Instead of writing the JSON data to a file, we can even write it to a string, and read it back from a string as shown below:

```
import json
lst = [10, 20, 30, 40, 50, 60, 70, 80, 90]
tpl = ('Ajay', 23, 2455.55)
dct = { 'Anil' : 24, 'Ajay' : 23, 'Nisha' : 22}

str1 = json.dumps(lst)
str2 = json.dumps(tpl)
str3 = json.dumps(dct)
l = json.loads(str1)
t = tuple(json.loads(str2))
d = json.loads(str3)
print(l)
print(t)
print(d)
```

- 's' in **dumps( )** and **loads( )** stands for string.

- It is possible to serialize/deserialize nested lists and directories as shown below:

```
# serialize/deserialize a dictionary
import json
lofl = [10, [20, 30, 40], [ 50, 60, 70], 80, 90]
f = open('data', 'w+')
json.dump(lofl, f)
f.seek(0)
inlofl = json.load(f)
print(inlofl)
f.close( )
```

```
# serialize/deserialize a dictionary
import json
contacts = { 'Anil': { 'DOB' : '17/11/98', 'Favorite' : 'Igloo' },
             'Amol': { 'DOB' : '14/10/99', 'Favorite' : 'Tundra' },
             'Ravi': { 'DOB' : '19/11/97', 'Favorite' : 'Artic' } }
f = open('data', 'w+')
json.dump(contacts, f)
f.seek(0)
incontacts = json.load(f)
print(incontacts)
f.close( )
```

Serialization of User-defined Types

- Standard Python types can be easily converted to JSON and vice-cersa. However, if we attempt to serialize a user-defined type to JSON we get following error:

  TypeError: Object of type 'Complex' is not JSON serializable

- To serialize user-defined types we need to define encoding and decoding functions. This is shown in the following program where, we serialize **Complex** type.

```
import json

def encode_complex(x):
    if isinstance(x, Complex) :
        return(x.real, x.imag)
    else :
```

```
        raise TypeError('Complex object type is not JSON serializable')

def decode_complex(dct):
    if '__Complex__' in dct :
        return Complex(dct['real'], dct['imag'])
    return dct

class Complex :
    def __init__(self, r = 0, i = 0) :
        self.real = r
        self.imag = i

    def print_data(self) :
        print(self.real, self.imag)

c = Complex(1.0, 2.0)
f = open('data', 'w+')
json.dump(c, f, default = encode_complex )
f.seek(0)
inc = json.load(f, object_hook=decode_complex )
print(inc)
```

- To translate a **Complex** object into JSON, we have defined an encoding function called **encode_complex( )**. We have provided this function to **dump( )** method's **default** parameter. **dump( )** method will use **encode_complex( )** function while serializing a **Complex** object.

- In **encode_complex( )** we have checked whether the object received is of the type **Complex**. If it is then we return the **Complex** object data as a tuple. If not, we raise a **TypeError** exception.

- During deserialization when **load( )** method attempts to parse an object, instead of the default decoder we provide our decoder **deconde_complex( )** through the **object_hook** parameter.

File and Directory Operations

- Python lets us interact with the underlying file system. In the process we can perform many file and directory operations.

- File operations include creation, deletion, renaming, copying, checking if an entry is a file, obtaining statistics of a file, etc.

- Directory operations include creation, recursive creation, renaming, changing into, deleting, listing a directory, etc.

- Path operations include obtaining the absolute and relative path, splitting path elements, joining paths, etc.

- '.' represents current directory and '..' represents parent of current directory.

- Given below is a program that demonstrates some file, directory and path operations.

```
import os
import shutil

print(os.name)
print(os.getcwd( ))
print(os.listdir('.'))
print(os.listdir('..'))

if os.path.exists('mydir') :
    print('mydir already exists')
else :
    os.mkdir('mydir')

os.chdir('mydir')
os.makedirs('.\\dir1\\dir2\\dir3')
f = open('myfile', 'w')
f.write('Having one child makes you a parent...')
f.write('Having two you are a referee')
f.close( )
stats = os.stat('myfile')
print('Size = ', stats.st_size)

os.rename('myfile', 'yourfile')
shutil.copyfile('yourfile', 'ourfile')
os.remove('yourfile')

curpath = os.path.abspath('.')
os.path.join(curpath, 'yourfile')
if os.path.isfile(curpath) :
    print('yourfile file exists')
```

else :
    print('yourfile file doesn\'t exist')

Problem 16.1

Write a program to read the contents of file 'messages' one character at a time. Print each character that is read.

Program

```
f = open('messages', 'r')
while True :
    data = f.read(1)
    if data == '' :
        break
    print(data, end ='')

f.close( )
```

Output

You may not be great when you start, but you need to start to be great.
Work hard until you don't need an introduction.
Work so hard that one day your signature becomes an autograph.

Tips

- **f.read(1)** reads 1 character from a file object **f**.

- **read( )** returns an empty string on reaching end of file.

- if **end=''** is not used, each character read will be printed in a new line.

Problem 16.2

Write a program that writes four integers to a file called 'numbers'. Go to following positions in the file and report them.

10 positions from beginning
2 positions to the right of current position
5 positions to the left of current position
10 positions to the left from end

Program

```
f = open('numbers', 'wb')
f.write(b'231')
f.write(b'431')
f.write(b'2632')
f.write(b'833')
f.close( )
f = open('numbers', 'rb')
f.seek(10, 0)
print(f.tell( ))
f.seek(2, 1)
print(f.tell( ))
f.seek(-5, 1)
print(f.tell( ))
f.seek(-10, 2)
print(f.tell( ))
f.close( )
```

Output

```
10
12
7
1
```

Problem 16.3

Write a Python program that searches for a file, obtains its size and reports the size in bytes/KB/MB/GB/TB as appropriate.

Program

```
import os

def convert(num) :
    for x in ['bytes', 'KB', 'MB', 'GB', 'TB']:
        if num < 1024.0:
            return "%3.1f %s" % (num, x)
        num /= 1024.0

def file_size(file_path):
```

```
    if os.path.isfile(file_path):
        file_info = os.stat(file_path)
        return convert(file_info.st_size)

file_path = r'C:\Windows\System32\mspaint.exe'
print(file_size(file_path))
```

Output

6.1 MB

Problem 16.4

Write a Python program that reports the time of creation, time of last access and time of last modification for a given file.

Program

```
import os, time

file = 'sampledata'
print(file)

created = os.path.getctime(file)
modified = os.path.getmtime(file)
accessed = os.path.getatime(file)

print('Date created: ' + time.ctime(created))
print('Date modified: ' + time.ctime(modified))
print('Date accessed: ' + time.ctime(accessed))
```

Output

```
sampledata
Date created: Tue May 14 08:51:52 2019
Date modified: Tue May 14 09:11:59 2019
Date accessed: Tue May 14 08:51:52 2019
```

Tips

- Functions **getctime( )**, **getmtime( )** and **getatime( )** return the creation, modification and access time for the given file. The times are returned as number of seconds since the epoch. Epoch is considered to be 1st Jan 1970, 00:00:00.

- **ctime( )** function of **time** module converts the time expressed in seconds since epoch into a string representing local time.

 **Exercise**

[A] State whether the following statements are True or False:

(a) If a file is opened for reading, it is necessary that the file must exist.

(b) If a file opened for writing already exists, its contents would be overwritten.

(c) For opening a file in append mode it is necessary that the file should exist.

(a) On opening a file for reading which of the following activities are performed:

    1. The disk is searched for existence of the file.
    2. The file is brought into memory.
    3. A pointer is set up which points to the first character in the file.
    4. All the above.

(b) Is it necessary that a file created in text mode must always be opened in text mode for subsequent operations?

(c) While using the statement,

    fp = open('myfile.', 'r')

    what happens if,

      — 'myfile' does not exist on the disk
      — 'myfile' exists on the disk

(d) While using the statement,

    f = open('myfile', 'wb')

    what happens if,

      — 'myfile' does not exist on the disk
      — 'myfile' exists on the disk

(e) A floating-point array contains percentage marks obtained by students in an examination. To store these marks in a file 'marks.dat', in which mode would you open the file and why?

[B] Attempt the following:

(a) Write a program to read a file and display its contents along with line numbers before each line.

(b) Write a program to append the contents of one file at the end of another.

(c) Suppose a file contains student's records with each record containing name and age of a student. Write a program to read these records and display them in sorted order by name.

(d) Write a program to copy contents of one file to another. While doing so replace all lowercase characters to their equivalent uppercase characters.

(e) Write a program that merges lines alternately from two files and writes the results to new file. If one file has less number of lines than the other, the remaining lines from the larger file should be simply copied into the target file.

(f) Write a program to encrypt/decrypt a file using:

(1) Offset cipher: In this cipher each character from the source file is offset with a fixed value and then written to the target file.

For example, if character read from the source file is 'A', then write a character represented by 'A' + 128 to the target file.

(2) Substitution cipher: In this cipher each for character read from the source file a corresponding predetermined character is written to the target file.

For example, if character 'A' is read from the source file, then a '!' would be written to the target file. Similarly, every 'B' would be substituted by '5' and so on.

(g) Suppose an Employee object contains following details:

employee code
employee name
date of joining
salary

Write a program to serialize and deserialize this data.

(h) A hospital keeps a file of blood donors in which each record has the format:

Name: 20 Columns
Address: 40 Columns
Age: 2 Columns
Blood Type: 1 Column (Type 1, 2, 3 or 4)

Write a program to read the file and print a list of all blood donors whose age is below 25 and whose blood type is 2.

(i) Given a list of names of students in a class, write a program to store the names in a file on disk. Make a provision to display the nth name in the list, where **n** is read from the keyboard.

(j) Assume that a Master file contains two fields, roll number and name of the student. At the end of the year, a set of students join the class and another set leaves. A Transaction file contains the roll numbers and an appropriate code to add or delete a student.

Write a program to create another file that contains the updated list of names and roll numbers. Assume that the Master file and the Transaction file are arranged in ascending order by roll numbers. The updated file should also be in ascending order by roll numbers.

(k) Given a text file, write a program to create another text file deleting the words "a", "the", "an" and replacing each one of them with a blank space.

17 Miscellany

- Miscellany

- Command-line Arguments

- Parsing of Command-line

- Bitwise Operators

- Assertion

- Inner Functions

- Decorators

- Decorating Functions with Arguments

- Unicode

- bytes Datatype

- Programs

- Exercise

The topics discussed in this chapter are far too removed from the mainstream Python programming for inclusion in the earlier chapters. These topics provide certain useful programming features, and could prove to be of immense help in certain programming strategies.

Command-line Arguments

- Arguments passed to a Python script are available in **sys.argv**.

```
# sample.py
import sys
print('Number of arguments recd. = ', len(sys.argv))
print('Arguments recd. = ', str(sys.argv))
```

If we execute the script as

C:\>sample.py cat dog parrot

we get the following output

Number of arguments recd. = 4
Arguments recd. = sample.py cat dog parrot

- If we are to write a script for copying contents of one file to another, we can receive source and target filenames through command-line arguments.

```
# filecopy.py
import sys, getopt
import shutil

argc = len(sys.argv)
if argc != 3 :
    print('Incorrect usage')
    print('Correct usage: filecopy source target')
else :
    source = sys.argv[1]
    target = sys.argv[2]
    shutil.copyfile(source, target)
```

Parsing of Command-line

- While using the 'filecopy.py' program shown above, the first filename is always treated as source and second as target. If we wish to have flexibility in supplying source and target filenames, we can use options at command-line:

  filecopy.py -s phone -t newphone
  filecopy -t newphone -s phone
  filecopy -h

- To permit this flexibility, we should use the **getopt** module to parse the command-line.

```
# filecopy.py
import sys, getopt
import shutil

if len(sys.argv) == 1 :
    print('Incorrect usage')
    print('Correct usage: filecopy.py -s <source> -t <target>')
    sys.exit(1)

source = ''
target = ''
try:
    options, arguments = getopt.getopt(sys.argv[1:],'hs:t:')
except getopt.GetoptError:
    print('filecopy.py -s <source> -t <target>')
else :
    for opt, arg in options :
        if opt == '-h':
            print('filecopy.py -s <source> -t <target>')
            sys.exit(2)
        elif opt == '-s' :
            source = arg
        elif opt == '-t' :
            target = arg
        else :
            print('source file: ', source)
            print('target file: ', target)
            if source and target :
                shutil.copyfile(source, target)
```

- The **getopt( )** method parses **sys.argv[1:]** and returns a sequence of (option, argument) pairs and a sequence of non-option arguments.

- **-h** option is for help about usage of the program.

- **sys.exit( )** terminates the execution of the program.

Bitwise Operators

- Bitwise operators permit us to work with individual bits of a byte. There are many bitwise operators available:

  ~ - Complement
  << - left shift, >> - right shift
  & - and, | - or, ^ - xor

- Bitwise operators usage:

  ```
  ch = 32
  dh = ~ch      # toggles 0s to1s and 1s to 0s
  eh = ch << 3   # << shifts bits in ch 3 positions to left
  fh = ch >> 2   # >> shifts bits in ch 2 positions to right
  a = 45 & 32    # and bits of 45 and 32
  b = 45 | 32    # or bits of 45 and 32
  c = 45 ^ 32    # xor bits of 45 and 32
  ```

- Remember:

  Anything ANDed with 0 is 0.
  Anything ORed with 1 is 1.
  1 XORed with 1 is 0.

- Bitwise operators purpose :

  ~ - Converts 0 to 1 and 1 to 0
  << >> - shift out desired number of bits from left or right
  & - Check whether a bit is on / off. Put off a particular bit
  | - Put on a particular bit
  ^ - Toggle a bit

- <<= >>= &= |= ^= - Bitwise compound assignment operators

- **a = a << 5** is same as **a <<= 5**.

- Except ~ all other bitwise operators are binary operators.

```
def show_bits(n) :
    for i in range(32, -1, -1) :
        andmask = 1 << i
```

```
        k = n & andmask
        print('0', end = '') if k == 0 else print('1', end = '')

show_bits(45)
print( )
print(bin(45))
```

On execution of this program, we get the following output:

```
00000000000000000000000000101101
0b101101
```

- This program prints binary equivalent of 45, by calling **show_bits( )** function. **show_bits( )** performs a bitwise and operation with individual bits of 45, and prints a 1 or 0 based on the value of the individual bit.

Assertion

- An assertion allows you to express programmatically your assumption about the data at a particular point in execution.

- Assertions perform **run-time checks** of assumptions that you would have otherwise put in code comments.

```
# denominator should not be zero
avg = sum(numlist) / len(numlist)
```

Instead of this, a safer way to code will be:

```
assert len(numlist) != 0
avg = sum(numlist) / len(numlist)
```

If the condition following **assert** is true, program proceeds to next instruction. If it turns out to be false then an **AssertionError** exception occurs.

- Assertion may also be followed by a relevant message, which will be displayed if the condition fails.

```
assert len(numlist) != 0, 'Check denominator, it appears to be 0'
avg = sum(numlist) / len(numlist)
```

- Benefits of Assertions:

- Over a period of time comments may get out-of-date. Same will not be the case with assert, because if they do, then they will fail for legitimate cases, and you will be forced to update them.

- Assert statements are very useful while debugging a program as it halts the program at the point where an error occurs. This makes sense as there is no point in continuing the execution if the assumption is no longer true.

- With assert statements, failures appear earlier and closer to the locations of the errors, which make them easier to diagnose and fix.

Inner Functions

- An inner function is simply a function that is defined inside another function. Following program shows how to do this:

```
# outer function
def display( ) :
    a = 500
    print ('Saving is the best thing...')

    # inner function
    def show( ) :
        print ('Especially when your parents have done it for you!')
        print(a)

    show( )

display( )
```

On executing this program, we get the following output:

```
Saving is the best thing...
Especially when your parents have done it for you!
500
```

- **show( )** being the inner function defined inside **display( )**, it can be called only from within **display( )**. In that sense, **show( )** has been encapsulated inside **display( )**.

- The inner function has access to variables of the enclosing function, but it cannot change the value of the variable. Had we done **a = 600** in **show( )**, a new local **a** would have been created and set, and not the one belonging to **display( )**.

Decorators

- Functions are 'first-class citizens' of Python. This means like integers, strings, lists, modules, etc. functions too can be created and destroyed dynamically, passed to other functions and returned as values.

- First class citizenship feature is used in developing decorators.

- A decorator function receives a function, adds some functionality (decoration) to it and returns it.

- There are many decorators available in the library. These include the decorator **@abstractmethod** that we used in Chapter 14.

- Other commonly used library decorators are **@classmethod**, **@staticmethod** and **@property**. **@classmethod** and **@staticmethod** decorators are used to define methods inside a class namespace that are not connected to a particular instance of that class. The **@property** decorator is used to customize getters and setters for class attributes.

- We can also create user-defined decorators, as shown in the following program:

```
def my_decorator(func) :
    def wrapper( ) :
        print('****************')
        func( )
        print('~~~~~~~~~~~~~~~~~')
    return wrapper

def display( ) :
    print('I stand decorated')

def show( ) :
    print('Nothing great. Me too!')

display = my_decorator(display)
display( )
show = my_decorator(show)
```

show( )

On executing the program, we get the following output.

```
****************
I stand decorated
~~~~~~~~~~~~~~~~~~~
****************
Nothing great. Me too!
~~~~~~~~~~~~~~~~~~~
```

- Here **display( )** and **show( )** are normal functions. Both these functions have been decorated by a decorator function called **my_decorator( )**. The decorator function has an inner function called **wrapper( )**.

- Name of a function merely contains address of the function object. Hence, in the statement

  display = my_decorator(display)

  we are passing address of function **display( )** to **my_decorator( )**. **my_decorator( )** collects it in **func**, and returns address of the inner function **wrapper( )**. We are collecting this address back in **display**.

- When we call **display( )**, in reality **wrapper( )** gets called. Since it's inner function, it has access to variable **func** of the outer function. It uses this address to call the function **display( )**. Before and after this call, it prints a pattern.

- Once a decorator has been created, it can be applied to multiple functions. In addition to **display( )**, we have also applied it to **show( )** function.

- The syntax of decorating **display( )** is a complex for two reasons. Firstly, we have to use the word display thrice. Secondly, the decoration gets a bit hidden away below the definition of the function.

- To solve both the problems, Python permits usage of @ symbol to decorate a function as shown below:

```
def my_decorator(func) :
    def wrapper( ) :
```

```
        print('****************')
        func( )
        print('~~~~~~~~~~~~~~~~~~')
    return wrapper

@my_decorator
def display( ) :
    print('I stand decorated')

@my_decorator
def show( ) :
    print('Nothing great. Me too!')

display( )
show( )
```

Decorating Functions with Arguments

- Suppose we wish to define a decorator that can report time required for executing any function. We want a common decorator which will work for any function regardless of number and type of arguments that it receives and returns.

```
import time

def timer(func) :
    def calculate(*args, **kwargs) :
        start_time = time.perf_counter( )
        value = func(*args, **kwargs)
        end_time = time.perf_counter( )
        runtime = end_time - start_time
        print(f'Finished {func.__name__!r} in {runtime:.8f} secs')
        return value
    return calculate

@timer
def product(num) :
    fact = 1
    for i in range(num) :
        fact = fact * i + 1
    return fact

@timer
```

```
def product_and_sum(num) :
    p = 1
    for i in range(num) :
        p = p * i + 1

    s = 0
    for i in range(num) :
        s = s + i + 1

    return (p, s)

@timer
def time_pass(num) :
    for i in range(num) :
        i += 1

p = product(10)
print('product of first 10 nos.=', p)
p = product(20)
print('product of first 20 nos.=', p)
fs = product_and_sum(10)
print('product and sum of first 10 nos.=', fs)
fs = product_and_sum(20)
print('product and sum of first 20 nos. =', fs)
time_pass(20)
```

Here is the output of the program...

```
Finished 'product' in 0.00000770 secs
product of first 10 nos.= 986410
Finished 'product' in 0.00001240 secs
product of first 20 nos.= 330665665962404000
Finished 'product_and_sum' in 0.00001583 secs
product and sum of first 10 nos.= (986410, 55)
Finished 'product_and_sum' in 0.00001968 secs
product and sum of first 20 nos. = (330665665962404000, 210)
Finished 'time_pass' in 0.00000813 secs
```

- We have determined execution time of three functions—**product( )**, **product_and_sum( )** and **time_pass( )**. Each varies in arguments and return type. We are still able to apply the same decorator **@timer** to all of them.

- The arguments passed while calling the 3 functions are received in ***args** and ****kwargs**. This takes care of any number of positional arguments and any number of keyword arguments that are needed by the function. They are then passed to the suitable functions through the call

  value = func(*args, **kwargs)

- The value(s) returned by the function being called is collected in **value** and returned.

- Rather than finding the difference between the start and end time of a function in terms of seconds a performance counter is used.

- **time.perf_counter( )** returns the value of a performance counter, i.e. a clock in fractional seconds. Difference between two consecutive calls to this function determines the time required for executing a function.

- On similar lines it is possible to define decorators for methods in a class.

Unicode

- Unicode is a standard for representation, encoding, and handling of text expressed in all scripts of the world.

- It is a myth that every character in Unicode is 2 bytes long. Unicode has already gone beyond 65536 characters.

- In Unicode every character is assigned an integer value called code point, which are usually expressed in Hexadecimal.

- Code points for A, B, C, D, E are 0041, 0042, 0043, 0044, 0045. Code points for characters अआइईउ of Devanagari script are 0905, 0906, 0907, 0908, 0909.

- Computers understand only bytes. So we need a way to represent Unicode code points as bytes in order to store or transmit them. Unicode standard defines a number of ways to represent code points as bytes. These are called encodings.

- There are different encoding schemes like UTF-8, UTF-16, ASCII, 8859-1, Windows 1252, etc. UTF-8 is perhaps the most popular encoding scheme.

- The same Unicode code point will be interpreted differently by different encoding schemes.

- Code points 0041 maps to byte value 41 in UTF-8, whereas it maps to byte values ff fe 00 in UTF-16. Similarly, code point 0905 maps to byte values e0 a4 85 and ff fe 05 \t in UTF-8 and UTF-16 repsectively. You may refer table available at https://en.wikipedia.org/wiki/UTF-8 for one to one mapping of code points to byte values.

- UTF-8 uses a variable number of bytes for each code point. The higher the code point value, the more bytes it needs in UTF-8.

bytes Datatype

- In Python text is always represented as Unicode characters and is represented by **str** type, whereas, binary data is represented by the **bytes** type. You can create a **bytes** literal with a prefix **b**.

```
s = 'Hi'
print(type(s))
print(type('Hello'))
b = b'\xe0\xa4\x85'
print(type(b))
print(type(b'\xee\x84\x65'))
```

will output

```
<class 'str'>
<class 'str'>
<class 'bytes'>
<class 'bytes'>
```

- We can't mix **str** and **bytes** in concatenation, in checking whether one is inside another, or while passing one to a function that expects the other.

- Strings can be encoded to bytes, and bytes can be decoded back to strings as shown below:

```
eng = 'A B C D'
dev = 'अअइ ई'

print(type(dev))
print(type(eng))
```

```
print(dev)
print(eng)

print (eng.encode('utf-8') )
print (eng.encode('utf-16') )
print (dev.encode('utf-8') )
print (dev.encode('utf-16') )

print(b'A B C D'.decode('utf-8'))
print(b'\xff\xfeA\x00 \x00B\x00 \x00C\x00 \x00D\x00'.decode('utf-16'))
print(b'\xe0\xa4\x85 \xe0\xa4\x86 \xe0\xa4\x87
\xe0\xa4\x88'.decode('utf-8'))
print(b'\xff\xfe\x05\t \x00\x06\t \x00\x07\t \x00\x08\t'.decode('utf-
16'))

<class 'str'>
<class 'str'>
अअइ ई
A B C D
b'A B C D'
b'\xff\xfeA\x00 \x00B\x00 \x00C\x00 \x00D\x00'
b'\xe0\xa4\x85 \xe0\xa4\x86 \xe0\xa4\x87 \xe0\xa4\x88'
b'\xff\xfe\x05\t \x00\x06\t \x00\x07\t \x00\x08\t'
A B C D
A B C D
अअइ ई
अअइ ई
```

- How these Unicode code points will be interpreted by your machine or your software depends upon the encoding scheme used. If we do not specify the encoding scheme, then the default encoding scheme set on your machine will be used.

- We can find out the default encoding scheme by printing the value present in **sys.stdin.encoding**. On my machine is set to UTF-8.

- So when we print **eng** or **dev** strings, the code points present in the strings are mapped to UTF-8 byte values and characters corresponding to these byte values are printed.

Problem 17.1

Write a program that displays all files in current directory. It can receive options -h or -l or -w from command line. If -h is received display help about the program. If -l is received, display files one line at a time,. If -w is received, display files separated by tab character.

Program

```
# mydir.py
import os, sys, getopt

if len(sys.argv) == 1 :
    print(os.listdir('.'))
    sys.exit(1)

try:
    options, arguments = getopt.getopt(sys.argv[1:],'hlw')
    print(options)
    print(arguments)
    for opt, arg in options :
        print(opt)
        if opt == '-h':
            print('mydir.py -h -l -w')
            sys.exit(2)
        elif opt == '-l' :
            lst = os.listdir('.')
            print(*lst, sep = '\n')
        elif opt == '-w' :
            lst = os.listdir('.')
            print(*lst, sep = '\t')
except getopt.GetoptError:
    print('mydir.py -h -l -w')
```

Output

```
C:\>mydir  -l
data
messages
mydir
nbproject
```

numbers
numbersbin
numberstxt
sampledata
src

Problem 17.2

Windows stores date of creation of a file as a 2-byte number with the following bit distribution:

left-most 7 bits: year - 1980
middle 4 bits - month
right-most 5 bits - day

Write a program that converts 9766 into a date 6/1/1999.

Program

```
dt = 9766
y = (dt >> 9) + 1980
m = (dt & 0b111100000) >> 5
d = (dt & 0b11111)
print(str(d) + '/' + str(m) + '/' + str(y))
```

Output

6/1/1999

Tips

• Number preceded by 0b is treated as a binary number.

Problem 17.3

Windows stores time of creation of a file as a 2-byte number. Distribution of different bits which account for hours, minutes and seconds is as follows:

left-most 5 bits: hours
middle 6 bits - minute
right-most 5 bits - second / 2

Write a program to convert time represented by a number 26031 into 12:45:30.

Program

```
tm = 26031
hr = tm >> 11
min = (tm & 0b11111100000) >> 5
sec = (tm & 0b11111) * 2
print(str(hr) + ':' + str(min) + ':' + str(sec))
```

Output

12:45:30

Problem 17.4

Write assert statements for the following with suitable messages:

- Salary multiplier sm must be non-zero
- Both p and q are of same type
- Value present in num is part of the list lst
- Length of combined string is 45 characters
- Gross salary is in the range 30,000 to 45,000

Program

```
# Salary multiplier m must be non-zero
sm = 45
assert sm != 0, 'Oops, salary multiplier is 0'

# Both p and q are of type Sample

class Sample :
    pass

class NewSample :
    pass

p = Sample( )
q = NewSample( )
assert type(p) == type(q), 'Type mismatch'

# Value present in num is part of the list lst

num = 45
lst = [10, 20, 30, 40, 50]
```

assert num in lst, 'num is missing from lst'

Length of combined string is less than 45 characters

s1 = 'A successful marriage requires falling in love many times...'
s2 = 'Always with the same person!'
s = s1 + s2
assert len(s) <= 45, 'String s is too long'

Gross salary is in the range 30,000 to 45,000

gs = 30000 + 20000 * 15 / 100 + 20000 * 12 / 100
assert gs >= 30000 and gs <= 45000, 'Gross salary out of range'

Problem 17.5

Define a decorator that will decorate any function such that it prepends a call with a message indicating that the function is being called and follows the call with a message indicating that the function has been called. Also, report the name of the function being called, its arguments and its return value. A sample output is given below:

Calling sum_num ((10, 20), { })
Called sum_num ((10, 20), { }) got return value: 30

Program

```
def calldecorator(func) :
    def _decorated(*arg, **kwargs) :
        print(f'Calling {func.__name__} ({arg}, {kwargs})')
        ret = func(*arg, **kwargs)
        print(f'Called {func.__name__} ({arg}, {kwargs}) got ret val: {ret}')
        return ret

    return _decorated

@calldecorator
def sum_num(arg1,arg2) :
    return arg1 + arg2

@calldecorator
def prod_num(arg1,arg2) :
    return arg1 * arg2
```

```
@calldecorator
def message(msg) :
    pass

sum_num(10, 20)
prod_num(10, 20)
message('Errors should never pass silently')
```

Output

Calling sum_num ((10, 20), { })
Called sum_num ((10, 20), { }) got return value: 30
Calling prod_num ((10, 20), { })
Called prod_num ((10, 20), { }) got return value: 200
Calling message (('Errors should never pass silently',), { })
Called message (('Errors should never pass silently',), { }) got return value: None

 **Exercise**

[A] State whether the following statements are True or False:

(a) We can send arguments at command line to any Python program.

(a) The zeroth element of the sys.argv is always the name of the file being executed.

(b) An inner function can be called from outside the outer function.

(c) An inner function has access to variables created in outer function.

(d) In Python a function is treated as an object.

(e) A function can be passed to a function and can be returned from a function.

(f) A decorator adds some features to an existing function.

(g) Once a decorator has been created, it can be applied to only one function within the program.

(h) It is mandatory that the function being decorated should not receive any arguments.

(i)   It is mandatory that the function being decorated should not return any value.

(j)   Type of 'Good!' is bytes.

(k)   Type of msg in msg ='Good!' is str.

[B] Answer the following:

(a)   Write a program using command line arguments to search for a word in a file and replace it with the specified word. The usage of the program is shown below.

C:\> change -o oldword -n newword -f filename

(b)   Write a program that can be used at command prompt as a calculating utility. The usage of the program is shown below.

C:\> calc <switch> <n> <m>

Where, **n** and **m** are two integer operands. **switch** can be any arithmetic operator. The output should be the result of the operation.

(c)   Rewrite the following expressions using bitwise compound assignment operators:

a = a | 3   a = a & 0x48   b = b ^ 0x22
c = c << 2   d = d >> 4

(d)   Consider an unsigned integer in which rightmost bit is numbered as 0. Write a function **checkbits(x, p, n)** which returns True if all "n" bits starting from position "p" are turned on, False othewise. For example, **checkbits(x, 4, 3)** will return true if bits 4, 3 and 2 are 1 in number **x**.

(e)   Write a program to receive a number as input and check whether its 3rd, 6th and 7th bit is on.

(f)   Write a program to receive an integer as input and then exchange the contents of its 2 bytes using bitwise operators.

(g)   Write a program to receive a 8-bit number into a variable and then exchange its higher 4 bits with lower 4 bits.

(h)   Write a program to receive a 8-bit number into a variable and then set its odd bits to 1.

(i)   Write a program to receive a 8-bit number into a variable and then check if its 3rd and 5th bit are on. If these bits are found to be on then put them off.

(j)   Write a program to receive a 8-bit number into a variable and then check if its 3rd and 5th bit are off. If these bits are found to be off then put them on.

Index

237